WEATHER WISDOM

WEATHER WISDOM

❧

*Being an Illustrated Practical Volume
Wherein Is Contained Unique Compilation and
Analysis of the Facts and Folklore
of Natural Weather Prediction*

by
ALBERT LEE

❧

With 30 Edifying Illuminations Executed by
William C. Sherb

Promulgated and Published by
DOUBLEDAY & COMPANY, INC., GARDEN CITY, NEW YORK
In Anno Domini 1976, the Leap Year
and Valid for All the Years Thereafter

Library of Congress Cataloging in Publication Data

Lee, Albert, 1942-
Weather wisdom.

Includes index.
1. Weather forecasting. 2. Weather lore. I. Title: Weather wisdom.
QC995.L36   551.6′31
ISBN 0-385-11016-2
LIBRARY OF CONGRESS CATALOG CARD NUMBER 75-40733

*To my wife, Carol, without whose help
this book would not have been written.
And to my children, Laura and Christopher,
without whose interference this book
would have been written much sooner.*

CONTENTS

INTRODUCTION

"What's in it for me?" is the slightly cynical, yet typically American, reaction to an unlearned subject. It is no mere coincidence that the only philosophy founded on this continent is, in fact, pragmatism. So in presenting this book on weather wisdom, I am compelled to justify its worth, its practical value.

That's easy. *Weather Wisdom* is a basic text on the art of observation forecasting. With it, an individual can make surprisingly accurate short-range weather predictions. For all of us who look for our moment in the sun—the hunter, the sailor, the sports participant or spectator, the gardener, or just the backyard barbecue enthusiast—being able to make on-the-spot weather predictions is, in itself, of real value.

But being weather-wise means more than never getting rained on. It means being sensitive to nature. The weather-wise individual is aware of the color and texture of the heavens, the dew on the grass, the flight of birds, the chirping of crickets, and the very taste of the wind. These are the indicators on which an observation forecast is made. The subtle changes that take place in our environment all have meanings. They are effects of changes, and if carefully read, can foretell additional changes. To practice weather wisdom is to nurture a high degree of sensitivity to the environment—in a sense, to regain the heritage we have somehow lost in a man-made world of synthetics, mortar, and steel. And the practical value of that? Well, I believe William Cullen Bryant said it best:

> To him who in the love of Nature
> holds communion with her visible forms,
> she speaks a various language.

Those who developed our rich stock of weather sayings and proverbs, of course, had no such idealized notions of their relationship with nature. They were practical Yankees engaged in a working partnership with nature. To forecast nature was not a matter of choice, but pure necessity. The weather determined when to sail, when to sow, when to forage, and when to venture out into the wilderness. As Ben Franklin put it: "Some are weatherwise, some are otherwise. . . ." Or, as Cornwall put it: "Those who are weather-wise are seldom otherwise." For the otherwise usually lost out.

This book is intended to be at once a practical manual of weather forecasting and a short course in sensitivity training. It will present, in simple terms, the basics of modern meteorological understanding, along with those ancient weather signs that have proven to be fairly reliable. With this understanding will come an expanded awareness of your environment, and of the intricate ordering of nature. As you sensitize yourself to nature's activities, you enrich sensual satisfaction with every outing and derive an almost mystical pleasure from your weather wisdom. John Ruskin captured this value when he wrote in 1839 about the then infant art of meteorology:

> It is the science of the pure air and the bright heaven, its thoughts are amidst the loveliness of creation, it leads the mind as well as the eye to the morning mist, the noonday glory and the twilight cloud, to the purple peace of the mountain heaven, to the cloudy repose of the green valley; now expatiating on the silence of stormless aether, now on the rushing of the wings of the wind. It is indeed a knowledge which must be felt to be in its very essence full of the soul of the beautiful.

WEATHER WISDOM

CHAPTER ONE

⟡

Folklore or Fact?

"You can't fly that little plane in a thunderstorm, can you?" an old-timer at the airport asked as I prepared my single-engine plane for a long-awaited flight into Canada. "No," I said, "but there isn't going to be any storm." I had listened to the morning weather report and only minutes earlier received my briefing from the nearest U. S. Weather Bureau Flight Service Station. All signs pointed to clear flying.

"Robins are in the bush," the old man said; "that's where they perch before a storm." I ignored the cracker-barrel philosophizing and took off, but I hadn't gotten three thousand feet above the runway before I spotted the black-bellied cumulus clouds closing in. I made a hasty retreat back to the airport. The old-timer was waiting at the hangar. "Come back to perch?" he said in true told-ya-so fashion.

That was my baptism into weather wisdom. An old man—who probably had never even heard of meteorology—had made a more accurate prediction than the U. S. Weather Bureau with its hodgepodge of sophisticated measuring equipment. Why? Because he was sensitive to something that they weren't: that robins, sensing a storm's approach, always seek shelter in bushes before it breaks. As a pilot and as a writer who is fond of feigning sensitivity, it was knowledge I had to know more about. I wrote to all fifty state climatologists and found rather matter-of-fact acceptance of the skill the old man used. Some called it "weather lore predicting," others described it as "observation forecasting," and one climatologist simply said the old man was "weather-wise."

By taking cues from the skies, from the activities of birds and insects, from the trees and flowers, from the dew on the ground, the taste of the air, the chirping of crickets, from aching bones, and from a thousand other indicators not found in the climatologist's handbook, one can make surprisingly accurate short-range forecasts. In fact, a weather-wise person can be more precise at times than the U. S. Weather Bureau. Why? Because the bureau's prognosis is made for a large area and over twelve to thirty-six-hour periods. The weather-wise person is taking his reading from nature right now, and right on the spot that affects him. It's immediate, and it works.

There's absolutely nothing new about the art of observation forecasting. If it were a profession, it would probably be older than that often-alluded-to oldest profession. Earliest records of weather lore date back six thousand years. It was, in fact, among man's earliest attempts to make cause-effect relationships between the elements in his environment. Nothing happened that did not have a cause and effect. The actions of birds before a storm, for example, could be linked with the storm that soon overwhelmed the skies. The striking of flint could be linked to the flame that issued forth. There was, man discovered, an order to existence.

On this order the ancient Egyptians planned their lives on the assumptions embodied in their weather lore. Aristotle wrote of weather lore in his work "On Meteors." One of Aristotle's star pupils, Theophrastus, devoted a major portion of his life to assembling weather wisdom into orderly presentations. Theophrastus' *Inquiry into Plants and Minor Works on Odours and Weather*

2

Signs contains many worthwhile weather insights as valid today as they were when he wrote them in the fourth century B.C. Aratus, a Greek poet and astronomer, whom St. Paul called "one of your own poets," put his weather insights into verse. His work, *Prognostica,* will be quoted frequently throughout this book because it is both eloquent and profound.

This apparent natural ordering of weather is found throughout our literary heritage as well. Virgil wrote of weather in *Georgics.* Shakespeare's plays and sonnets abound with weather insights. And our earliest English ancestors centered literary attention on weather, such as in the Old English poem, *Beowulf,* which, if I can recall the symbolic interpretation from suffering through its contorted language, is about the sun-god, who struggles with the forces of winter and is eventually destroyed for his efforts.

Religious writers embraced weather prediction, too. The Greek god Zeus and his Roman counterparts Jupiter Pluvius and Jupiter Tonans, gods of rain and thunder, started it off. The Old and New Testaments of the Christian Bible are thoroughly laced with weather wisdoms. The writings of Job are richest on this score. A single example from the Bible should illustrate the significance of such sayings and also shed some light on the universality of many of these natural observations. Jesus Christ said to the Pharisees (Matthew 16:2, 3):

"When it is evening, ye say, it will be fair weather: for the sky is red. And in the morning, it will be foul weather today: for the sky is red and lowering.

"O ye hypocrites, ye can discern the face of the sky; but can ye not discern the signs of the times?"

Could the Pharisees discern the face of the sky? Well, the weather deduction based on the coloration of the sky at dawn and dusk was, as we shall see in later chapters, an accurate one. This same prediction can be found in the chants of European mariners:

> Red sky in morning, sailors take warning.
> Red sky at night, sailors delight.

Or from Shakespeare's poem *Venus and Adonis:*

A red morn: that ever yet betokened
Wreck to the seamen, tempest to the field,
Sorrow to shepherds, woe unto the birds,
Gust and foul flaws to herdsmen and to herds.

Or in the saying of Midwestern American farmers:

Evening red, morning gray
Sets the traveler on his way;
Evening gray, morning red,
Brings down rain upon his head.

Remarkably similar, weather lores such as these are found in
virtually every culture, in every part of the world. Many are set
in rhymes and poetic stanzas. Peter Farb, in his book *Word Play*,
says that probably all speech communities use verse because it
aids memory. That is not unique to weather lore—Hindus, Greeks,
and Latin philosophers all used verse for many scientific statements. As late as the nineteenth century the Japanese used verse
for parts of state documents, and, of course, religious orders have
continued to use verse and chants to glorify their sacred doctrines.
A hundred-year-old tombstone from a Skaneateles, New York,
graveyard illustrates the significance of rhyme better than I can.
It was inscribed:

Underneath this pile of stones
Lies all that's left of Sally Jones
Her name was Briggs; it was not Jones,
But Jones was used to rhyme with stones!

Rhymes both grave and merry have made information easier to
remember and communicate to others, and the lore of earlier
peoples was therefore assisted in passage from one generation
to the next.

Until the twentieth century everyone took these bits of weather
wisdom in all seriousness, for life depended on their predictions.
If misguessed, sailors were caught by storms with sails fluttering,
farmers were caught with sustenance crops still unharvested,

hunters would miss their game, and merchants would be stranded on roads that were barely passable even in good weather. Weather lore was serious business to these people whose livelihoods depended on the whims of nature. It was, in fact, all the security they had to live by.

This was especially true when man first traversed the land that is now America. He found a land marked by contrasting weather, a land where temperatures ranged from −70 degrees Fahrenheit in Montana to 130 degrees in California, and where rainfall varied from 150 inches a year in the Washington State area to less than ten inches in the deserts of Arizona. It was a continent where hurricanes, tornadoes, and blizzards were commonplace. As was change. Mark Twain once said that he counted 136 different kinds of weather in New England—all in twenty-four hours. Yet in Maine they say that there are only two seasons: "Winter and July." With such extremes, both the red man and, later, the European settler found weather prediction essential. North America, with a relatively short history, quickly developed one of the greatest stores of weather lore anywhere, as people from all corners of the earth not only brought weather lore with them, but found plenty of occasion to make use of it in the New World.

And for those of you who feel weather prognostics are quaint, but of little relevance in our climate-controlled twentieth century, think again. The modern shipper takes great pains to estimate weather, for if he is caught in port unable to load or unload because of nature, he loses about five thousand dollars a day. On the Mississippi River, predicting the water level can make a major profit and loss difference, since every inch of draught on the cargo barges means more than a hundred dollars in increased grain-carrying capacity. Modern farmers continue to be at the mercy of changing weather. If a farmer can predict when the first frost will come, for instance, he can maximize his yield. Construction men must also know the varieties of temperature, since concrete can't be poured when the mercury falls below freezing. And even industries as far-flung as textiles must predict the length and strength of seasons. A cool September, for instance, can double

5

the sales of winter coats, while a warmer-than-average September can practically eliminate such sales. Obviously, the clothmakers, the tailors, and the storekeepers must second guess weather even today.

Anticipating weather is as vitally needed today as it was in the past, perhaps even more so, since modern production and transportation scheduling is dependent on timetables never before as rigid or critical. But most of us have turned our responsibility for prediction over to laboratory meteorologists. This has probably come about because of our spiritual belief in modern science and in our rejection of the mythologies of the past. This is, of course, a misunderstanding of what weather wisdom is. Weather lore is considered a branch of folklore. It was passed from generation to generation by word of mouth, often in rhymes, just like folklore. But there the comparison should cease. For folklore is based on superstitions, fears, and misconceptions. It has little to offer the scientific world (though it is of great value to all of us curious about our heritage and common humanity). Much weather lore (but by no means all) is based on generations of careful observation of the environment and is therefore as worthy of consideration as any space-age hypothesis. Consider Ecclesiastes (1:6, 7):

> The wind goeth toward the south and turneth about unto the north; it whirleth about continually, and the wind returneth again according to his circuits. All the rivers run into the sea; yet the sea is not full; unto the place from whence the rivers come, thither they return again.

The point is that there is a consistency in nature, a predictable pattern. The observations of the Greek weather, written down in the fourth century B.C., still hold firm for modern-day Greece. Eric Sloane, perhaps the greatest living authority on American weather lore, points out that family almanacs in his collection that were written a hundred years ago are accurate indications of current weather patterns. Because of this consistency, both the early Greek and modern Idaho farmer can plant crops and predict their chances of maturation. Because of consistency, there is an order on which the infant science of climatology and meteorology could be based.

Meteorology and weather lore forecasting have a common heritage. They examine the same phenomena and differ mostly in the indicators used. The meteorologist consults a few instruments and some tables of accumulated data to make his prognosis; the weather-wise person uses dozens of more subtle, yet more readily available, indicators at the same moment. Dr. Edward Jenner, the eighteenth-century English doctor who developed the first successful vaccination for smallpox, presents an excellent example of diverse weather-wise indicators in the following rhyme:

SIGNS OF RAIN

The hollow winds begin to blow,
The clouds look black, the grass is low;
The soot falls down, the spaniels sleep,
And spiders from their cobwebs peep.
Last night the sun went pale to bed,
The moon halos hid her head;
The boding shepherd heaves a sigh,
For see, a rainbow spans the sky.
The walls are damp, the ditches small,
Closed is the pink-eyed pimpernel.
Hark how the chairs and tables crack!
Old Betty's nerves are on the rack;
Loud quacks the duck, the peacocks cry,
The distant hills are seeming nigh.
How restless are the snorting swine,
The busy flies disturb the kine,
Low o'er the grass the swallow wings,
The cricket, too, how sharp he sings!
Puss on the hearth, with velvet paws,
Sits wiping o'er her whiskered jaws;

7

Through the clear streams the fishes rise,
And nimbly catch the incautious flies.
The glowworms, numerous and light,
Illumined the dewy dell last night;
At dusk the squalid toad was seen,
Hopping and crawling o'er the green;
The whirling dust the wind obeys,
And in the rapid eddy plays;
The frog has changed his yellow vest,
And in a russet coat is dressed.
Though June, the air is cold and still,
The mellow blackbird's voice is shrill;
My dog, so altered in his taste,
Quits mutton bones on grass to feast;
And see yon rooks, how odd their flight!
They imitate the gliding kite,
And seem precipitate to fall,
As if they felt the piercing ball.
'T will surely rain; I see with sorrow,
Our jaunt must be put off to-morrow.

Though Dr. Jenner wrote his poem two hundred years ago in England, most of the indicators can be seen any June day in Kansas (or any similar northern latitude) as a front approaches, bringing rain with it. Or consider another Englishman, Jonathan Swift, who gave yet another poetic evaluation of a closely akin setting in *Rain:*

Careful observers may foretell the hour
By sure prognostics when to dread a shower.
While rain depends, the pensive cat gives o'er
Her frolics and pursues her tail no more;
Returning home at night you'll find the sink
Strike your offended sense with double stink.
If you be wise, then go not far to dine,
You'll spend in coach-hire more than save in wine.

8

A coming shower your shooting corns presage,
Old aches will throb your hollow tooth with rage.
Sauntering in coffee-house is Dulman seen;
He damns the climate and complains of spleen.
Meanwhile the South, rising with dobbled wings,
A sable cloud athwart the welkin flings,
That swilled more liquor than it could contain,
And, like a drunkard, gives it up again.
Brisk Susan whips her linen from the rope,
While the first drizzling shower is borne aslope.
Such is that sprinkling which some careless quean
Flirts on you from her mop, but not so clean.
You fly, invoke the gods; then, turning, stop
To rail; she singing still, whirls on her mop.
Not yet the dust had shunned the unequal strife,
But, aided by the wind, fought still for life,
And wafted with its foe by violent gusts,
'Twas doubtful which was rain and which was dust.
Ah! where must needy poet seek for aid
When dust and rain at once his coat invade?

Modern scientists, both climatologists and biologists, far from dismissing these observations, have learned much from them. The robin nesting before a storm, for example, has been given some study. Two reasons are given by biologists, each equally feasible. First, the low-pressure air which accompanies a storm is not as dense as high-pressure air and therefore is harder for birds to fly in. Second, some birds' nests, robins, for one, are so frail that they would be destroyed if the birds were not in them during storms. Nature has programmed storm sensitivity into these birds, and biologists have learned about birds from such acts. Another example was given to me by Robert Orton, Texas State climatologist. He recalls a recent conversation with a rancher who had been watching the weather for thirty years. "The rancher," Orton says, "observed over the years that high clouds, primarily cirrus and alto-cumulus, streaming in from the southwest often precede rain in southwestern Texas. It was not until weather satellites that professional meteorologists realized that significant amounts of moisture invaded southern and western Texas from the Pacific Ocean via northern Mexico. Most meteorologists had assumed that the Gulf of Mexico was the only significant moisture source for Texas." The rancher was right, the pros wrong.

Not all weather lore is true, of course. As is often the case with orally transmitted knowledge, the original observation may have been well rooted in fact, but as it was passed down, the facts eroded, especially if the recipients were not weather watchers and therefore didn't re-evaluate the statements.

Also, as man moved across the face of the earth, he took his weather lore with him. While it was applicable to the place from which he came, it may not hold water in his new location. Seafarers, for example, made their weather predictions at many latitudes in both the Northern and Southern hemispheres, and these predictions often must be carefully scrutinized before applying to a given locale. Yet most of the weather lore that has reached us is either of European origin or native American, and since the weather patterns in both locations have similarities, they can be applied.

Since observation forecasting has become mixed with folklore and legend as it was passed down, some of it is blatantly false. In the Ozark Mountains, for example, Eliot Wigginton had his students gather folk wisdom from their parents and grandparents. They came up with such gems as: "A bad winter is betide, if hair grows thick on a bear's hide," or "Bad winter is ahead if muskrat lodges have more logs." More to the truth would be that extra-heavy animal coats are a better indicator that the previous summer was a good one, and the same applies to the sturdier muskrat lodge that was a product of fine weather for building. Causative predictions are equally foolhardy, such as the provincial Chinese belief that igniting small red firecrackers would bring rain, or the American slave belief that killing a snake brought rain. (Everyone today knows that the only thing that is sure to bring on showers is washing and waxing your car, or hanging out a wash to dry.)

Many of the weather sayings that make absolute predictions have a religious connotation. It is said, for example, that:

> If it rains on St. Swithin's Day [July 15],
> It will rain for forty days straight.

As the story goes, there was a delay of forty days duration in moving the body of St. Swithin from one sepulcher to his permanent resting place. Until he was finally laid to rest, the rain came down continuously. Such a statement is based on a belief in miracles, not in natural processes, and can be dismissed on those grounds. But even further, the calendar has been reformed since St. Swithin died, so July 15 today has little bearing on the July 15 of the early Julian calendar.

And finally, there are weather lore sayings that, while accurate enough, are not easily applied to the modern environment, such as the Zuni Indian statement that, "When the hair is wet in the scalping tent, surely it will rain."

Weather wisdom, as presented in the following chapters, will present weather lore that is either true or may have enough basis in truth to warrant consideration. It will ignore the tens of thousands of weather lore predictions based on superstitions and religion that could more properly be classified as folklore. It is designed, not to compete with the U. S. Weather Bureau or with the scientific methods of modern forecasting, but to augment it. By understanding the basis of modern forecasting (presented in Chapter Two), along with the effects changing weather has on your immediate environment, you can become more sensitive than either the person who knows only his laboratory instruments or the old-timer who knows only the signs of the sky. The more input the better, as C. L. Prince wrote: "Do not neglect any of these signs, for it is good to compare a sign with another sign. If two agree, have hope, but be assured still more by a third."

But don't expect absolute accuracy. There are some instances when signs fail. The mariner, for example, says "anything can happen in unsettled weather," and the farmer says "all signs fail in times of drought." But even in normal weather periods, "absolute" and "weather forecast" are not interchangeable terms. The great shortfall in weather lore's history is that it has been recorded by human beings who are anxious to find precision, absolute dependability, and universal meaning in their truths. Totally unanticipated weather can appear from the wrong direction, carrying the wrong ingredients, and at the wrong time of year. Even the U. S. Weather Bureau scores only 85 per cent accuracy in anticipating the actions of major weather fronts. That 85 per cent accuracy isn't bad, considering the bureau's efforts are credited in saving upwards of three billion dollars a year from property damage and crop washouts. But they have had the good sense to anticipate the unexpected by including hedging words, such as "possibility" and "probability." You can take the bureau's fairly good information, crank in the subtle bits of data from observation forecasting, and possibly even improve on their score. You can't be right all the time—nature simply doesn't allow it—but you can be pretty close to the mark, at least a lot closer than the author of this untitled eighteenth-century Bedfordshire village poem recorded by Richard Inwards:

> "Well, Duncombe, how will be the weather?"
> "Sir, it looks cloudy altogether,
> And coming across our Houghton Green,
> I stopped and talked with old Frank Beane.
> While we stood there, sir, old Jan Swain
> Went by and said he knowed 'twould rain;
> The next that came was Master Hunt,
> And he declared he knew it wouldn't.
> And then I met with Farmer Blow,
> He plainly said he didn't know,
> So, sir, when doctors disagree,
> Who's to decide it, you or me?"

CHAPTER TWO

୧৵৵৹

Whether It's Science . . .

What you are about to read is privileged information. It is the meteorological explanation of weather workings, and, as such, it is privileged to those born in the last century or so. Those who wrote the weather lore embodied in this book did not have the benefit of understanding these larger concepts—of cyclonic motion, of source regions, of hydrometers, and, for most, not even of barometers. They did not have the benefit of consulting the latest weather photograph flashed down by radio waves from a satellite. The weather-wise simply read the signs, and from them made fairly accurate predictions, just as many can read the face of a clock without understanding the concept of "time" or can drive and repair a car without the vaguest understanding of the thermodynamics on which the internal combustion engine is based.

You, too, could become a weather midwife without ever attending an anatomy class. Indeed, most of the books written on weather lore waste no time in explaining the overriding concepts of weather. But a little bit of learning, despite what

Alexander Pope said, is a very good thing. It can expand the sensitivity of the observation forecaster and make him or her less provincial. It's much like the story of the astronaut who ran off course and landed, not knowing in which country, or continent, he was. He saw a man standing in a field nearby and asked, "Where am I?" "Why," the man said, "you're in Old Sam's wheat field." A broader view would have been helpful.

The grand-scale concepts of weathermaking are really quite elementary, once the specialized language and subtle details are stripped away. To begin with, weather is nothing more than the result of collisions between huge blobs of air, called air masses. Like colossal dodgem cars they rush about, and wherever they smack together, they produce the radical changes that we know as weather. Yet unlike the pell-mell movement of dodgem cars, air masses follow clear-cut courses.

Air masses are moved on their courses by the wind. And what moves the wind? Two things: First, there's the heating of air by the sun. Hot air moves toward cold, and cold air is drawn to heat. This means that the air at the equator is heated and begins heading north; when it gets into the Arctic Circle, it's cooled off and turns around for a journey back to the equator. If that was all there was to it, all wind would move directly from north to south

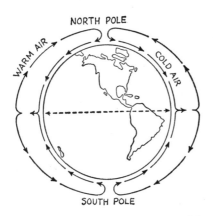
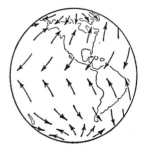

and back again. But the second factor, the earth's rotation on its axis, modifies the wind. It creates a veering off of the north-to-south course. In the Northern Hemisphere this has the effect of nearly all wind moving from the west to the east. In the Southern Hemisphere, wind generally moves from the east westward. In most of the United States and southern Canada, any change from the prevailing west winds (a west wind being one that blows *from* the west) is likely to bring foul weather. Thus the American folk poem:

> When the wind is in the north,
> The skillful fisher goes not forth;
> When the wind is in the east,
> 'Tis good for neither man nor beast;
> When the wind is in the south,
> It blows the flies in the fish's mouth;
> But when the wind is in the west,
> There it is the very best.

In the United States the wind is seldom directly out of the west. In the summer the wind is southwesterly and in the winter northwesterly. But any westerly wind is considered to most probably be associated with pleasant weather. And since people are pleased by good weather, there is a belief among Midwestern farmers that one should do all winter business when the wind is northwesterly.

The air masses, those blobs of air, are formed in one of several source regions, then move out with the wind to power them and the prevailing patterns to steer the course. But while the air mass sat in the source region, it picked up the physical characteristics of that location, just as a non-smoker's clothes will pick up the odor of cigarettes after spending some time in a room where people are smoking. Or another example of this adopting of surroundings can be found in a wine cellar. The air is stagnant in the cellar, and it's obvious that it has acquired both the dampness from the cellar walls and the mustiness of the dusty enclosure. So an air mass that started up above polar waters will be cold and wet, while one that started over continental land in the polar region would be cold and dry. Those that start in the tropics are obviously warm, and the ones born over water obviously damp. Meteorologists give these air masses fancy names that refer to their origin, such as Tropical Maritime (mT) and Polar Continental (cP), but such names are not important. What is important is to understand that air masses differ in temperature and moisture content and that you can tell the air-mass child by taking a look at the parent region from which it came. By watching weather reporters on television news programs you can get an idea of which air masses most often come to your area. For example, the cold, dry mass that forms over the north-central part of Canada has the largest single effect in weather in the central and eastern portions of the United States.

You can even get more basic and say that there are really only two kinds of air masses: warm and cold. These two do not mix, and when they meet, there's a fight for control that can be seen and felt by thunderstorms, snow, hail, rain, and high winds sometimes resulting in tornadoes and hurricanes. Naturally, since an air mass is moving in a direction, it has a front. And it is along these fronts, sometimes thousands of miles wide, that the collision between warm and cold air masses takes place. And the entire trick of observation-weather forecasting is to be able to decide which one of these two air masses will strike your location, when, and with what force. And since fronts don't always produce extreme weather, it becomes quite a trick at times.

The cold-front storm is the one to fear. It strikes with all the subtlety of a twelve-pound sledge hammer. The most violent storms come with cold fronts: they give the shortest time warning of an approach and are past most quickly. The warm-front weather is just the opposite. Precipitation with a warm front is generally mild. The warm front gives lots of warning as it moves in, yet, like a slow-moving southern gentleman, usually stays longer, bringing the mild, yet long-duration rains. Thus the weather wisdom:

16

Rain long foretold, long last;
Short notice, soon will past.

or

Small showers last long,
but sudden storms are short.

Shakespeare, *Richard III*

A warm front moves about half as fast as a cold front, and it gradually pushes the cooler air before it back, and one can predict its coming from one to three days ahead of time. Warm air, being lighter than cool air, rides up over as it moves in a very gradual incline. Thus, if you could slice a warm front crosswise, you would see that it looks like a wedge moving backward across the land. As the warm air is forced up, it cools; water is condensed and may fall as rain or snow. If you had plenty of time to sit and watch the warm front moving in, you would notice that the clouds generally keep getting lower and lower over an extended period until the front arrives, often with rain. This begins first with the high cirrus wispy clouds, little clouds called mares' tails. Then the stratus clouds start moving in. They are flat, gray, and unexciting in appearance, and they usually cover the sky in what is known as a leaden sky. The rain, probably drizzle, finally passes

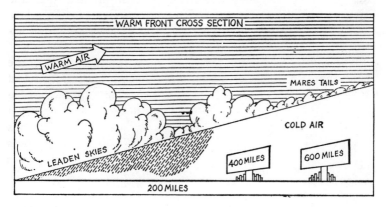

17

with the front and, almost as slowly as it arrived, the front moves on. Behind the warm front you will experience warmer, more humid air with dingy, yet gradually clearing skies.

Worth noting here is that warm and cold are relative terms. On a summer day a cold front can have temperatures in the 70-degree range, for instance, which is still cold in comparison to the air in the warm front, with temperatures in the 80-degree bracket. It is easier to remember this if you think of them as "warm*er*" fronts and "cold*er*" fronts, meaning they are warmer or colder than the air mass they are attempting to invade.

As the first indicator of the warm front is the cirrus, or mares' tails clouds, the earliest indicator of cold-front storms is a mackerel sky. Mackerel clouds (actually alto-cumulus clouds) look like herds of little white puffs moving across the otherwise beautifully clear sky. Thus the mariners' advice:

> Mares' tails and mackerel scales,
> Make lofty ships carry low sails.

After the mackerel skies comes a sudden buildup of cumulus clouds. These are the lovely white fluffy clouds which are usually associated with the clear skies and excellent visibility of cold air.

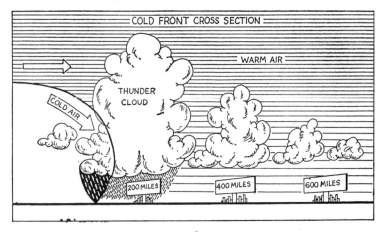

But when cumulus clouds pile up on a front, they make for dramatic, and violent, action. Inside the towering cumulus cloud the warm air is driven vertically up by the cold at phenomenal speeds. As it rises, it cools, condenses, then drives the rain down in torrents. If the upper portion of the cloud is cold enough, the rising rain crystallizes into hail, is dropped, but picked up again by the cloud's upcurrents, and when it gets near the top, receives another coating of ice, again and again until the balls of hail are too heavy and fall to earth. This upward and downward force can create hail as large as golf balls. The rapid motion inside the cloud also makes for a lot of static electricity, and lightning results. Damage from such a thunderstorm can be severe. Winds change as dramatically at the approach of a cold-front storm. In the Northern Hemisphere they will first change from westerly, to southwesterly, to southerly (the backing winds); then, when

19

the storm comes on top of you, the winds "veer" to easterly or
northerly.

> When the wind veers toward the sun,
> Trust it not for back 'twill run.

And, finally, the wind returns to westerly, which we already know
is best, and the storm subsides. As soon as the black-bottomed
tower cloud moves on, the sky turns clear, and the soft-looking,
delicate white clouds appear to foretell pleasant weather ahead.

That's essentially all there is to weather. Two kinds of fronts,
two distinct sets of cloud formations and conditions that accompany them. To be either a meteorologist or an observation forecaster, one has only to read these conditions in advance of the
event, just as a knowing parent can read the mischievous look
in a toddler's eye and know what he, or she, is about to do. The
meteorologist and observation forecaster have the same changes
as indicators—air pressure, temperature, humidity, wind speed,
and wind direction. The meteorologist reads these changes directly from his bank of instruments. The observation forecaster
may use a couple of instruments too, but most of the time he
does his reading from the effects those same changes have on
animals, plants, trees, and his own five (or six) senses. To learn
observation forecasting, it's best to start out with the meteorologist's basic tools as a backup. When a natural indicator is observed, it can then be evaluated with the instruments. Soon the
sensitive observer will be able to read the air pressure, humidity,
temperature, wind speed, and wind direction from the environment without mechanical aids. But even from the start, one need
not spend hundreds of dollars for a weather lab. The only essen-
tials are a thermometer, a barometer, and a piece of string to use
as a weather vane. A hygrometer is useful, but not necessary.

The barometer measures changes in air pressure, which is one
of the better indicators of altering weather. The air pressure is
actually the weight of the air above you at any given time.
Roughly fourteen to fifteen pounds per square inch of atmosphere
would be normal at sea level and given static conditions. (That's

about one ton of pressure for every square inch.) Naturally, since there is less air on top of you on Mount Everest, the weight, or air pressure, is lower, and if you were standing in a hole below sea level, the air pressure, or weight of air on you, is greater. But air doesn't always weigh the same. Warm air is lighter and weighs less, and wet air is lighter than dry air. (Water vapor actually weighs less than air.) So the pressure varies with changes in air temperature and humidity, or air wetness. How rapidly the air pressure, or barometric pressure, changes is an indicator of the kind and severity of weather anticipated.

The concept of air pressure is difficult for some to understand because neither air nor pressure can be seen. But it can be compared to a substance that acts remarkably similar and we can see —water. You are standing on the bottom of an ocean of air that acts much like the sea-water ocean. All of the weight of the water above you in the ocean is pressing down on you, creating pressure. The surface of the ocean is not stagnant. There are waves, constant peaks and valleys, that move across the surface above you. As a large wave goes over you, there is actually a mound of water overhead, and therefore more weight or pressure on you.

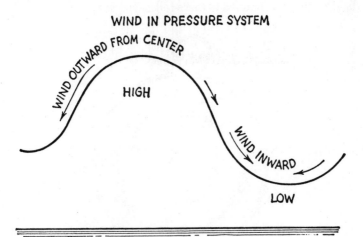

WIND IN PRESSURE SYSTEM

This mound, or wave, because it creates more pressure, is called a high-pressure area, or just plain *high*. When the valley between the mounds of waves passes over you, there is less weight or pressure, and therefore we have a low-pressure area, or *low*. Lows are huge, normally covering hundreds of miles. Highs are much smaller.

These high- and low-pressure centers create their own wind and have their own weather associated with them. Air rushes from an area of high pressure to an area of low pressure in nature's attempt to even out pressure. From a high, or mound, of pressure, the air flows away from the center, creating a wind in a clockwise direction. In a low, or depression, air flows inward, toward the bottom or center. This creates a wind that runs counterclockwise. Generally speaking, highs normally bring pleasant weather. Lows bring storms and unsettled conditions. The barometer, or "weatherglass," as it used to be called, is used to find out when the wave is moving over you, to measure whether the pressure overhead is increasing, indicating a high; decreasing, designating a low; remaining steady, indicating a continuation of the same weather; or changing abruptly up or down, showing unsettling conditions. A way to remember the significance of the direction is contained in these folk sayings:

ANEROID BAROMETER

CAPE COD BAROMETER

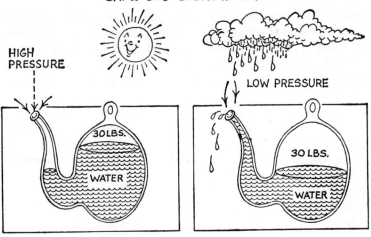

When the glass falls low,
Prepare for a blow;
When it rises high,
Let all your kites fly.
The hollow winds begin to blow,
The clouds look black, the glass is low.

First rise after low,
foretells stronger blow.

But just reading a barometer is about as useful as knowing the time on a broken wrist watch. What is being observed is change —how fast and in which direction—and therefore a monitoring system is needed. Using the aneroid barometer, the simplest kind available, you must set one hand on the other and watch every hour or so to see if the main indicator hand has moved up, meaning higher pressure, or down, meaning lower pressure.

Barometers have been used extensively by Europeans and sailors, but, oddly enough, the weather-wise American farmers seldom owned them, the one exception being Cape Codders, who invented their own brand of barometer. It was essentially a bottle with a long upward-turned spout, partially filled with water. When air pressure dropped, indicating bad weather, the water would be forced up the neck, indicating the change. When the pressure dropped significantly, the spout would spill over. Thus their statement: "When the glass spills over, so will the clouds."

There are many more natural barometers (that will be explained in later chapters). Chickweed, called the poor man's barometer, closes up when air pressure drops. Many kinds of waterfowl fly higher with lowering air pressure because it hurts their highly sensitive ears. And the increased pressure makes animals restless, furniture creak and moan, and people turn temperamental. Thus Dr. Jenner wrote:

> Hark how the chairs and tables crack!
> Old Betty's nerves are on the rack.
> . . . 'Twill surely rain; I see with sorrow,
> Our jaunt must be put off tomorrow.

Many of these weather lore indicators are as much an indication of increased humidity as a decrease in pressure. And humidity, or the percentage measurement of how full the air is with water, is critical to weather forecasting. As we have said, the temperature of the air determines how much water vapor it can

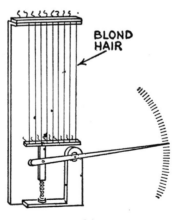

BLOND
HAIR

hold (warm holding more than cold). But no matter how large the bucket, it can't be any fuller than 100 per cent full, or it will spill over. Air can't be any fuller than 100 per cent humidity, or it too will spill over with rain or some other form of precipitation. Logically, then, if you have a day with 85 per cent humidity, and the temperature begins to drop on your thermometer (remember, colder air is a smaller water container), then the humidity will go up to 90, 95, 100 per cent and then spillage.

The devices used to determine increases in humidity or air saturation are called hygrometers (literally, water meters). The most basic is based on the weather folk knowledge that many fibers absorb moisture readily and shorten with increased humidity. Thus from Lieutenant A. P. Herbert's collection, *Weather Proverbs:*

> Curls that kink and cords that bind:
> Signs of rain and heavy winds.

Modern meteorologists haven't improved much on this folk wisdom, and, in fact, use "curls that bind" in one common hygrometer. The hair hygrometer uses blond hair specially treated to remove natural oils. The hairs are connected to a meter, and when they shrink or stretch with changing humidity, the degree of saturation is thus indicated. The weather-wise also use hemp rope, which does a fairly good job of absorbing moisture also. The Germans and Dutch have a variation for the mantle of homes called the "weather house." It is a little house with two doors. When it is going to rain, the man of the house appears holding an umbrella. When there is little humidity, the man goes back in, and the wife, usually holding a flower, comes out the other door. Inside this device is a strand of catgut, which, like the hair, absorbs moisture and tends to untwist; when dry it twists up tight. This movement is used to operate the actions of the weather people who pop in and out of the doors. As we shall see in later chapters, a lot of other substances in our environment absorb moisture and react, including human joints and bones; thus the aphorism, "It's gonna rain; I can feel it in my bones."

FAIR → ← RAIN

Another form of hygrometer is based on a principle no more sophisticated than that clothes hung out to dry in humid weather dry slower than in dry weather, and that when water evaporates it cools the surrounding area. Put these two concepts together and you can devise a wet-bulb thermometer. It is essentially just a wet cloth over the bulb of a conventional thermometer. When

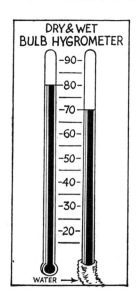

DRY & WET
BULB HYGROMETER

-90-
-80-
-70-
-60-
-50-
-40-
-30-
-20-

WATER →

the water evaporates, the temperature drops, and the reading can be made. This, however, has little meaning unless compared to a thermometer not in contact with the cloth. So we end up with two thermometers, one wet, one dry, and the difference in the reading of the two give us the spread, and thus the humidity.

For hundreds of years a similar rain forecaster employing salt has been used. Salt absorbs moisture, thus it weighs more before rain. Mariners soaked a piece of cloth in brine and let it dry. Thereafter, whenever the air turned damp, the cloth would also. And there is reportedly a stone in Finland, a fossil of potassium nitrate and rock salt, that is called the "weather stone." When humidity runs high, dark spots appear over the face of the rock, and nature is giving a hygrometer reading. From France comes a trinket that does the same thing. It is simply a piece of rag paper treated with chloride of cobalt. The paper is blue when dry, then, as humidity increases, changes to lilac and then to pink. The paper is cut into designs, such as a flower or woman with a full skirt, and it is hung in the house or car to give quick humidity readings and rain forecasts. These magic papers are still sold in great numbers in the United States as well as in France.

Relative humidity is expressed in another way that has even more meaning—dew point. The dew point is the temperature at which the air will no longer hold water, and some form of precipitation can be expected. It's another way of saying the temperature at which you reach 100 per cent humidity. If the dew point today is 38 degrees, for example, and the temperature is 41 degrees and falling, then you can expect some moisture to dampen your bonnet. Of course, the greater the spread of temperature between dew point and current temperature, the less chance of rain.

Dew point and dew should not be confused. Dew point is an indicator of how far the atmosphere is away from overflowing. Dew is the visible droplets of moisture that form on grass, plants, and metal objects in the morning. The Earl of Chesterfield described dew more poetically when he said, "The dews of the evening industriously shun, They're the tears of the sky for the

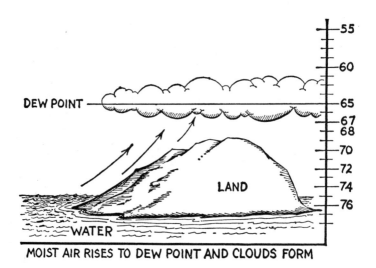

DEW POINT

55
60
65
67
68
70
72
74
76

LAND

WATER

MOIST AIR RISES TO DEW POINT AND CLOUDS FORM

loss of the sun." On the more scientific side, dew is formed when the air is chilled after sundown as the earth gives up its heat. To form dew, two conditions are necessary: lack of clouds, and a windless night. A cloud cover would hold down heat and not allow the drop in temperature of the grass needed for condensation. A night breeze would carry warm air over the ground, again preventing dew from forming. Morning dew thus comes with conditions that are right for a fair weather day, thus the oft-true prophecy:

> When the dew is on the grass,
> Rain will never come to pass.

And the opposite:

> When grass is dry at morning light
> Look for rain before the night.

In summer, fogs are formed in the same way as dew, on windless, cloudless nights, and thus are as much an indicator of good weather as dew. But in winter, fogs are often the result of warmer and wet air being blown over relatively cold land surfaces. These fogs are more apt to be harbingers of rain than fair skies. To remember the difference, the rhyme was devised:

A summer fog for fair,
A winter fog for rain:
A fact most everywhere,
In valley and on plain.

These same conditions give rise to these fog sayings:

When the mist creeps up the hill,
Fisher, out and try your skill;
When the mist begins to nod,
Fisher then put up your rod.

or

When fog goes up the rain is o'er,
When fog comes down 'twill rain some more.

Winter is the great immobilizer of man and machinery, which probably explains the profusion of winter weather lore. It also proves out the bromide that "an idle mind is the devil's workshop," since most winter indicators are devilishly inaccurate. While the few which will be included in this chapter do hold true, the vast majority (which will not be included) are flakier than the weather they vainly attempt to predict.

Most of the inaccurate winter lore comes from attempts to predict the entire season from a vantage point in the late fall or early winter. Such gems exist as: the width of the black band on the woolly bear caterpillar tells the severity of the coming winter, or that a heavy winter can be expected if there is a bumper crop of acorns for the squirrels, or the larger the beaver builds his house, the longer the winter will be. Most of these have little direct prognostic value (the few that do will be touched on in Chapter Nine), but it is thoroughly understandable how they came about. The farmer needed desperately to be able to determine the length and temperament of the winter, because it clearly indicated which crops would do best the following summer and how bountiful the harvest would be. Most of the predictors he came up with were more of a prayer for a long, constant winter that didn't end too early with crop-killing frosts. Snow that lies on the ground is fine for crops, or, as the Russian farmers said it: "Corn is as comfortable under snow as an old man is under his fur cloak." The less poetic Yankee simply said:

> Year of snow,
> Crops will grow.

Separating the farmer's wishful thinking from his weather wisdom, we find that he did have some ability to foretell snowfalls and general weather conditions a day or so before they changed. One of his favorite tools was his intuitive knowledge—also, well founded in scientific fact—that in subzero weather it is too cold to snow. The warmer the weather up to 32 degrees Fahrenheit, of course, the more chance of snow. Thus he watched for signs of cold:

> When the days begin to lengthen,
> The cold begins to strengthen.

And on clear nights:

> Cold is the night,
> When the stars shine bright.

The snow that did fall told the weather watcher what the temperature was like up above where the weather was brewing. Dry snowflakes meant that the atmosphere was moderately cold, while damp flakes meant temperatures were on the rise. From these he rightly concluded:

> When the snow falls dry it means to lie;
> But flakes light and soft bring rain oft.

> and

> Cut a snowball in half:
> Wet center means rain;
> Dry center can only be melted by the sun.

and

Snowflakes increasing in size,
Expect a thaw soon.

What farmers called a "hard winter" was actually a cold winter, and for some reason the Americans made it a contest to try and outdo folks from other areas on just how bitter cold it got in these parts. The topper of the lot has to go to the following Oregon account:

As I sat down one ev'nin' in a timber-town cafe,
A six-foot-seven waitress to me these words did say:
I see you are a logger and not a common bum,
For no one but a logger stirs his coffee with his thumb.
My lover was a logger. There's none like him today.
If you'd sprinkle whiskey on it, he'd eat a bale of hay.
He never shaved the whiskers from off his horny hide;
But he'd pound them in with a hammer, then bite 'em off inside.
My logger came to see me, one freezing winter day.
He held me in a fond embrace that broke three vertebrae.
He kissed me when we parted, so hard he broke my jaw,
And I could not speak to tell him he'd forgot his mackinaw.
I watched my logger lover going through the snow,
A-sauntering agily homeward at forty-eight below.
The weather tried to freeze him. It tried its level best.
At a hundred degrees below zero, he buttoned up his vest.
It froze clean down to China. It froze to the stars above.
At a thousand degrees below zero, it froze my logger love.
They tried in vain to thaw him. Then, if you'll believe me, sir,
They made him into ax blades to chop the Douglas fir.
That's how I lost my lover, and in this cafe I come
And here I wait till some one stirs his coffee with his thumb.
And then I tell my story of my love they could not thaw,
Who kissed me when we parted—so hard he broke my jaw.

Oregon Historical Quarterly

All of the cloud formations, wind changes, and life signs that indicate rain (in chapters Four, Six, and Seven) are roughly as pertinent to snowfall prediction—one of the major differences being that storm clouds in winter are not as dark. Weather watchers call winter storm clouds "snow blossoms" because they look much like delicate white flowers with a bluish tint. Also, the prevailing wind in winter is out of the northwest, and for most of this continent it brings cold, dry air. When it shifts to southwest winds, a thaw is predicted. And, naturally, when it turns around and comes at us from the east, violent weather may be in the offing. Snow's arrival, like the arrival of rain clouds, is marked by a general animation of man and beast, falling smoke, and many of the other general signs. There are few differences and even fewer of the anxieties associated with damaging spring and summer storms. Snow is greeted with much more acceptance by landsmen, as the Mediterranean expression puts it:

> With good wind, good bread, and peace at home,
> If snow does come, let it come.

In this chapter we have gone from blobs of air forming in the arctic to the Oregon chill factor—a long trip for such a short ex-

planation. To cover so much territory, the subject of what makes weather had to skip along the surface like a pebble on a pond and simplify to the point of making meteorologists cringe. If the subject was covered too rapidly for you, don't worry, it will be presented in other ways later. The pressure, humidity, and temperature variations will be seen in how they affect your daily environment, and you, and how you can read them through weather wisdoms. And the skies will speak more clearly to you than I can.

CHAPTER THREE

❦

Know Thyself

Sensitivity begins by dwelling within yourself, becoming aware of your own feelings and senses, then stretching outward with a reach that, hopefully, always "exceeds your grasp." Weather sensitivity, then, should begin with an evaluation of how weather affects your senses, your body, and even your emotional stability. Everything on the thin crust of this small planet is affected by weather, and you and I are no exceptions.

Climate affects all of our lives, directly and peripherally. Climate dictates the food available to us, the water we drink, the clothing and housing that shelters us, and the amount of energy our bodies are forced to give up or absorb. In the broadest sense, all human conduct is in some way touched by weather. This has led many theoreticians to develop deterministic concepts of society based on weather influences, just as Karl Marx formulated his theory of society on economic determiners. One of the most interesting of the weather determinists' theories was created by Baron de Montesquieu in his book *Esprit des lois*. Published in 1748, the work represented twenty years of comparisons between human characteristics and governments and the climates that acted upon them. Montesquieu concluded that inhabitants of cold countries had no real sensitivity to subtle tastes nor to wasteful emotion, while those who dwelled in warm lands appeared more sensitive and volatile. His examples were the phlegmatic English, compared to the emotional and aesthetic Italians. Montesquieu's conclusion was essentially that laws ought to be framed in accordance with the climates. Thus, in countries where wine has a more immediate effect due to weather, consumption should be restricted, and in countries where weather leads to lackadaisical behavior, laws should encourage the work ethic.

While interesting, such theories are far too broad to be of any real use and, of course, fall prey to stereotyping. Luckily, we need not go to Montesquieu's extremes to see how weather affects us. On the most basic level, your senses of sight, smell, and hearing are affected by changes in the weather. In a high-pressure area, air is relatively static and laden with dust, which reduces your visibility. But as a storm approaches, the atmosphere clears, and you can see more detail than normal. The thinning air before a storm makes distant objects appear nearer as well. Thus many local weather watchers pick out a distant hill or building on the horizon and look at it daily for clarity. When the object appears distant and hazy, then fair weather is ahead, but when it is crystal clear and close, rain can be expected soon. Mariners remembered this truism by chanting:

> The farther the sight,
> the nearer the rain.

Many have used this increased visibility to determine not only the onset of rain but the direction favorable and unfavorable winds would soon blow. Aristotle noted this in saying, "The cliffs and promontories of the shore appear higher and the dimensions of all objects seem larger, then the southeast wind is blowing." He could well have added, "and the rains will come." For wind direction does, in fact, provide a weather indicator, west winds usually bringing good weather in this hemisphere, and east winds bringing storms.

And when your eyes deceive you with a mirage, that, too, indicates a weather change. Sailors watch for mirages on the horizon and know from experience that when one appears, it means rain. When the mirage seems to grow larger or smaller, or bends out of shape, then that means a more extreme atmospheric condition, and, accordingly, he lowers his mainsails and prepares for a tempest.

Human sensitivity to smells is so far inferior to that of animals that if we had to depend on this sense to warn us of an approaching elephant stampede, then we would be underfoot by the time we were aware of any difference. Yet men do smell changes in weather. Sailors have even learned to navigate through dense fogs, literally following their noses. They can detect, for example, the difference between a sea breeze, which carries a heavy sea smell, and land breezes, with the smell of vegetation, flowers, and new-mown hay. One non-mariner, John Winthrop, wrote that after six weeks at sea he "smelled the sweet smell of a garden" when approaching the coastline.

Also, just before rain comes, your sense of smell will seem to improve. Everything will have a stronger odor, from the sweet scent of a flower to the putrid smell of a swamp. The fact is, the odors are repressed in a high-pressure center, and, as the bad-weather low moves in, the pressure is removed, and odors are allowed to escape.

> When the ditch and pond affect the nose,
> Then look out for rain and storm blows.

Your ears perk up as storms approach, too. "There is a sound of abundance of rain," Elijah said (1 Kings 18:41), and it is certainly true. There are a couple of theories on this phenomenon which you can choose from. One proposed by acoustical experts is that the dense cloud cover of a storm acts as a barrier, bouncing acoustical waves back toward earth, thus seemingly increasing sounds. Another is that when air is humid, there develops a homogeneity of the atmosphere. Cold air is warmed by condensation and warm air cooled by evaporation. Irregularities in air temperature interfere with acoustical waves, so when humidity eliminates these variations, sound levels go up. No one is certain which, if either, is correct, but there is truth in the saying:

> Sound traveling far and wide
> A stormy day will betide

> or

> When the forest murmurs and the mountain roars,
> Then close your windows and shut your doors.

If weather affects the human condition in various ways, then it must have an effect on our thinking and, to some extent, our behavior. Cicero believed it did when he wrote:

> The minds of men do in the weather share,
> Dark or serene as the day's foul or fair.

Changes in weather do affect our behavior. Consider first the obvious fact that weather changes mean changes in atmospheric pressure. Bad weather, you will recall, is associated with a falling barometer and lowering of the weight or pressure on each of us. Good weather is associated with a rising barometer, or high pressure. Changes in pressure affect your blood's chemistry, for it is pressure that forces the alertness-giving oxygen into your system. When the pressure lessens, the amount of oxygen forced into your blood lessens, and sluggishness sets in. Human beings, then, function best under pressure (a fact my editors have been telling me for years). There may also be a connection between atmospheric pressure and our overall energy level. Dr. Solomon Strouse writes of a yearlong study he conducted testing the blood-sugar levels of average people during different weather conditions. He concluded that blood-sugar levels are higher during high-pressure periods and lower during low-pressure weather. And blood-sugar levels are correlated with energy levels. Good weather, or high pressure, also means a lessening of humidity, and the negative

37

effect of humidity on human attitudes is well documented. High pressure seems to affect appetites as well, and it is a weather lore belief that when everything at the table is eaten, clear weather follows. And not to ignore the obvious, good weather means pleasant skies and opportunities for the children to play outside, a fact that reduces a different kind of pressure on most of us. Thus, it is obvious that we feel better when pressure is high and the skies are fair. As English King Alfred (in *Poems*) said more than a thousand years ago:

> So it falls that all men are
> With fine weather happier far.

And in Shakespeare's words (*Richard II*):

> Men judge by the complexion of the sky
> The state and inclination of the day.

The negative side of the coin is that the onset of bad weather can upset our equilibrium. Studies in both Europe and the United States over the past century have shown that the number of suicides increases during low-pressure, bad-weather periods. The Bank of England once maintained a policy of putting its most important books under lock and key during London fogs because too many bookkeeping errors occurred during these depressing (and depressive) conditions.

It has also been documented that excitability increases when pressure is low and humidity is high. Warring American Indian tribes used this fact of increased irritability to plan battles as storms approached; hence their prognosis that, "Storm gods give courage to the Red Man." And, from Virgil:

> Thus when the changeful temper of the skies
> The rare condenses, the dense rarefies,
> New motions on the altered air impress'd,
> New images and passions fill the breast.

Human attitudes are also affected by temperature. Any police department has records to prove the increase in crime during warm weather, and studies have also shown the increase in suicides and other anti-social behavior with high temperatures. It is no coincidence that the street riots in the United States have most often developed on July and August days, giving added dimension to the phrase "the long, hot summer." Or, as Shakespeare had Benvolio say in *Romeo and Juliet:*

> I pray thee, good Mercutio, let's retire:
> The day is hot, the Capulets abroad,
> And if we meet, we shall not 'scape a brawl,
> For now, these hot days, is the mad blood stirred.

One of the lengthiest studies ever conducted on the effects of temperature, humidity, and barometric readings in relation to abnormal behavior was completed in 1904 by social scientist Edwin G. Dexter. In his book *Weather Influences,* Dexter detailed his ten-year project in which the daily murder, suicide, assault, drunkenness, and school attendance records were compiled in New York City and in Denver, Colorado. Statistically comparing 600,000 separate behavioral deviations with U. S. Weather Bureau data, Dexter concluded that weather does distort rational behavior and is a factor in human misconduct. He also said there is a cutoff point where increased heat and humidity reduce social deviation. Dexter noted that assaults increased up to 85 degrees and thereafter dropped off sharply. Apparently, high temperatures increase irritability, but extremely high temperatures rob us of the energy to act out our weather-inspired hostilities.

You might argue that the effects of atmospheric pressure, humidity, and temperature on criminals, suicidal personalities, and those prone to street rioting are hardly indicative of weather's effects on more stable personalities. That may be true, though some effect is evident in most of us, even if we don't express it by jumping from buildings or clubbing others over the head. Weather, in fact, may even be said to affect us differently by economic class, since those that can afford it may insulate themselves with air conditioners and dehumidifiers in home, office, and car. If this is so, then the anonymous English writer who penned this poem may not have been far from the mark:

39

> The rain it raineth every day
> Upon the just and unjust feller,
> But mostly on the just, because
> The unjust hath the just's umbrella.

Besides general peevishness, the human body reacts with heightened discomfort, aches, and pains as low pressure and increased humidity precede bad weather. In one study of 367 arthritic patients, 72 per cent experienced increased pain each time the barometer fell. It is generally recognized that people who have rheumatic or arthritic problems, those with bad teeth, badly healed broken bones, stomach disorders, who are headache prone or have corns and bunions will experience aches and pains as humidity increases and pressure decreases. These unpleasant precursors of bad weather are frequently mentioned by the weatherwise:

> A coming storm your shooting corns presage,
> And aches will throb, your hollow tooth will rage.

Or from Theophrastus:

> If feet swell, the change will be to the south.

Or from Samuel Butler:

> As old sinners have all points
> o' th' compass in their bones and joints—
> Can by their pangs and aches find
> All turns and changes of the wind. . . .

If your bones do not signal changes of weather, you probably have some hair on your head to help you make predictions. Remember that the hygrometer, which meteorologists use to measure humidity, is operated by blond human hair. Your hair's disposition will change as rain approaches, too. If it is straight hair, it will feel lifeless as humidity increases, and if your hair is kinky and hard to manage normally, it will be worse, and you won't be able to do a thing with it before a storm. So the sayings go:

40

But I know ladies by the score
  Whose hair, like seaweed, scents the storm;
Long, long before it starts to pour
  Their locks assume a baneful form.

Lieutenant A. P. Herbert, R.N.V.

and Lieutenant Herbert again:

But when they hear the sibyl chant,
  "All colourless, and feels like clay,
All straight and horrible—I can't
  Do nothing with my hair today!"
Then write they down, "A deep depression runs
South-west from Iceland—secondary ones
  Are busy in the Bay."

Think of the powers of that young girl,
  And how much destiny must hinge
On whether she can get a curl
  To come in her confounded fringe!

You and I, then, are affected—perhaps even partially governed —by the weather. It has an influence on our perspective, on how we see, hear, and smell our surroundings. It may have an

41

influence on our moods. Certainly, anthropologists would not argue too vehemently against Charles Kingsley's tongue-in-cheek
analysis on weather's influence on man in *Ode to the North-East
Wind*:

> What is it molds the life of man?
>   The weather.
> What makes some black and others tan?
>   The weather.
>
> What makes the Zulu live in trees,
> And Congo natives dress in leaves
> While others go in furs and freeze?
>   The weather.
> 'Tis the hard grey weather
> Breeds hard English men.

❧❀❧

CHAPTER FOUR

Animal, Vegetable, and Mineral

In the animal kingdom, humans are the dullards. We haven't the vision of a buzzard, nor the sensitive nose of a basset hound. At birth we are pathetically underequipped compared to an ant, which, at first life, has every fact it needs for survival programmed into its nervous system, or a sparrow, that knows instinctively where its migratory existence will lead it. So if we humans, with our dulled senses and near-complete lack of instinct, can anticipate changes in our weather environment, it seems only logical that other living creatures can do so far better.

They can. For thousands of years shepherds, herdsmen, hunters, and fishermen have noted how the activities of animals, birds, insects, and fish change in anticipation of weather hours before human senses have received as much as a hint that something was happening. Naturally, such fine indicators were highly respected and became a major segment of the weather-wise individual's predictions.

The lowering pressure preceding a storm seems to stir animals to a variety of behavior patterns, but there are some general rules that must follow. Wild animals are seen to hunt food more diligently and eat more voraciously in anticipation of the long fast that will come while waiting out a storm. This instinct in some animals appears so great that they will take greater chances than normal to obtain food. Rabbits, for example, normally avoid box traps, but any farm boy will tell you that just before a snow or thunder storm, the catch of rabbits in box traps is spectacular.

For domestic animals an approaching storm seems to be marked by general nervous activity, but the patterns of that activity are more individualized than their more instinct-oriented cousins in the woods. One farmer said that his hound dog always scratched his left hind quarter against a post before a storm (perhaps the old dog's joints ached with humidity), and a sheep rancher concluded one ewe always rolled in dirt before it rained. The danger here, of course, is in making all-inclusive generalizations based on the behavior of one exceptional creature's actions, which is what I believe happened when the following weather sign was written:

> When a cow endeavors to scratch its ear,
> It means a shower is very near.
> When it thumps its ribs with angry tail,
> Look out for thunder, lightning, hail.

But even among domestic animals there are general signs of changing weather. Cattle and horses are said to bunch together before a storm, and, when a major storm approaches, they move down from the crests of hills into sheltered valleys. Sheep spring about in the fields just before weather clears. Cats wash their fur profusely before a storm, dogs act jittery, and bitches use the time to move their litters. Most domestic animals express extreme restlessness and put up more clatter than normal. For making noise before a storm, the jackass seems to be the most consistently vocal, thus the adage:

> When the ass begins to bray,
> Be sure we shall have rain that day.

44

The weather wisdom of the jackass made for one of Abe Lincoln's favorite anecdotes. Seems the local weather predictor in his home town of Springfield, Illinois, failed more often than not at second-guessing nature. Then one day a boy came to the mayor claiming that he could tell every time if a storm was going to approach. The mayor tried him out on several occasions and, sure enough, the boy was consistently right. The mayor was about to fire the old weatherman and instate the boy when the lad said he couldn't accept the position. "It's my jackass that does the predicting," he said. "Whenever a storm is buildin', he scratches his ear against the fence and brays terrible." So the mayor appointed the jackass instead. Abe would always pause at this point and say in a low tone, "That was the mayor's mistake." Why? everyone would ask Lincoln. "Because, ever since then jackasses have been seeking public offices." While the tale was meant as wit instead of wisdom, it nonetheless was acceptable in his day, as most farmers knew changing weather did affect their animals' behavior.

Of all the barnyard beasts, the pig has been given the most credit by farmers around the world as the weather sage. The ancient Greek lore written by Aratus says "swine in miry litter madly wallowing" is a sign of bad weather. Virgil, in telling the coming signs of storms, said, "Swine are not heedful to toss about with their snouts the loosened wisps." And while they are thrashing about, they are normally carrying a mouthful of straw, according to American and British husbandrymen. From Charles St. John's *Wild Sport in the Highlands* comes the passage: "It is proverbial that pigs see the wind; and they undoubtedly become restless and prepare their straw beds prior to a severe storm, some hours before human beings are aware of its approach." In nearly all European and American weather lore, swine are the only creatures that are consistently credited with "seeing the wind." This bit of folklore has been immortalized in the saying of Britons first recorded by Richard Inwards that:

> Grumphie smells the weather,
> An' grumphie sees the wun';

> He kens when clouds will gather,
> An' smoor the blinkin' sun.

Birds soar high on the list of weather sages, too. And for those city bound, they are one of the few animal indicators at hand, so they take on even greater significance. While most of the short-term bird indicators are verifiable, there is one set of beliefs that is totally fallacious, namely that birds foretell changes in seasons by when they migrate. Ornithologists don't have all the answers of why birds migrate, but they do know that many species conform to a timetable that follows a calendar far better than it coincides with actual seasonal weather variations. Some species, swifts, for instance, make their migrations on the same date every year. Others go when seeds and insects are no longer available, and often they misjudge their departures and are caught and killed by snow and ice storms. Tens of thousands of swallows were killed by a snowstorm while the birds were making their southern migration over France in the fall of 1939.

Many species of birds fly low to the ground before a storm. There are a number of reasons given for this behavior. First, birds (and bats) have sensitive ears, and the lowering of air pressure before a storm causes discomfort, so they fly at the level where pressure is highest, close to the ground. Second, birds fly on air currents, and in fair weather the convection currents are upward, helping birds climb, while during the period of an approaching storm, air currents are downward. Third, insect-eating birds fly where the insects are. The air currents before a storm keep flying insects near the earth or water, and swallows and other birds that catch their suppers on the wing fly at that level to catch them. The reverse of all this, of course, is also true: birds fly higher as good weather approaches, hence the predictions:

> When swallows fleet soar high and sport in air,
> He told us that the welkin would be clear.

> or

> When ground lark soar high on a cloudy day,
> Clearing skies will follow.

Other species—geese, gulls, crows, and robins among them—
do not like to fly at all before a storm, and this, too, becomes a
weather indicator. The one obvious reason to remain grounded
as mentioned earlier is that the thinning air which precedes a
storm is harder to fly in (ask any pilot for verification). Also,
some birds build fragile nests that would be destroyed if they
were not in them when the winds and rains came, so nature seems
to have included self-preservation instincts in these cases. The
robin is the most famous bird in this country for sticking close to
the nest before a storm:

> If the robin sings in the bush
> Then the weather will be coarse;
> If the robin sings on the barn,
> Then the weather will be warm.

And, like children who must stay in because a storm is coming, these perching birds tend to squawk about it. Geese honk
before a storm, crows are said to call for rain, the bobwhite calls
out, "More wet, more wet," and the woodpecker sets up a racket
pecking at the tree. Some of the more sedate birds simply busy
themselves by preening their feathers.

How accurate are these bird predictions? Well, New England
lobstermen who go out to sea in small boats are said to get up
early to watch the sea gulls and wild geese. If these birds fly out
to sea in the morning, the fisherman is confident that it is safe for
him to venture out also. If they fly inland or seek the shelter of a
cove, then the fisherman thinks twice about casting off. In Maine
they swear by the saying:

> Wild geese, wild geese going out to sea
> All fine weather it will be.

Among amphibians, the frog is most often mentioned as a
weather forecaster. Since he is found in nearly all countries,
nearly every weather lore has a saying about him. Be it from India, China, Japan, Greece, England, or America, they all agree
that when frogs croak excessively, it will rain soon. In India they
pin it down even more by saying that, "When the frog croaks in

the meadow, it will rain in three hours' time." In Germanic countries of Europe the green tree frog is used in the home as a substitute for a barometer. The frog is kept in a glass jar half filled with water. Inside the jar is a ladder. On days when the weather will be bad the frog stays in the water and croaks, but as he senses clearing weather, he ascends part way up the ladder, and, during ultra-fine weather, he is said to be found most often at the top of the ladder. This hardly seems as accurate as an aneroid barometer, but it does express the faith the German, Austrian, and Swiss people place in their frogs' predictions, and there certainly must be some truth to it, or the people would not continue to go to the trouble of catching these slithery barometers.

Fish, as a general rule, seem to be only mediocre weather predictors. Most weather lores say that just before it rains, fish tend to stay closer than normal to the water surface (possibly due to a change in pressure and therefore a change in oxygen content of the water). But fishermen argue over whether the coming rain makes fish bite more or less. Some say they refuse bait and opt instead to grab for the flies that come low to the water just before a storm. Others say fish bite best and put up more fight on the line when rain is coming. So it boils down to which fisherman's story you want to believe. There is, however, far more general agreement that with the approach of a major thundershower, fish become less active and refuse to bite. Since the worst storms come from lows with backing winds, the saying is common that:

> Fish bite the least,
> With wind in the east.

Dolphins and porpoises, or sea hogs as sailors call them, are included in the mariners' fish predictions even though they are mammals. If dolphins are seen in large numbers on the surface, chasing around the ship and acting as if at play, then the sailors say that a storm is coming. Some analysts believe this behavior is due to the electrically charged atmosphere accompanying a storm. Whatever the reason, there is general acceptance that porpoises do surface more before storms. And because they are seen preceding storms, sailors consider the porpoise an evil omen whenever he is seen.

During Britain's Great Exhibition of 1851, a Dr. Merryweather appeared with a "storm warning system," which was a jar with twelve leeches inside and a small bell that would ring when the leeches became active. He advocated that the British Government set up leech-warning stations along the coasts, weather-forecasting stations that could be totally depended on. This British scientist was not the only one who believed that the motion of leeches was a precise measurement of changing weather. For hundreds of years in Spain jars were kept with leeches as weather indicators. They were said to tell of a change from twelve to twenty-four hours before it arrived. And, unlike the tree frog, the leech communicates a number of different messages —nine messages in all, according to the Spanish saying. They are:

1. If the leech takes up a position in the bottle's neck, rain is at hand.
2. If he forms a half-moon, when he is out of the water and sticking to the glass, it is a sure sign of tempest.
3. If he is in continual movement, thunder and lightning are coming soon.

49

4. If he seems as if he were trying to raise himself from the surface of the water, there will be a change in the weather.
5. If he moves slowly close to one spot, cold weather is coming.
6. If he moves rapidly about, expect strong wind when he stops.
7. If he lies coiled up on the bottom, fine, clear weather is coming.
8. If he forms a hook, clear, cold weather is coming.
9. If he is in a fixed position, very cold weather is certain to follow.

Of all the creatures whose actions have meanings to the weather-wise, the insects are the most consistent. This is because insects do not vary from one of a kind to the next of that kind. They are totally non-thinking minicomputers whose every action or reaction throughout their brief existence is predetermined. Think of how much more absolute an entomologist can be than a human behavioral psychologist, and how much more dependable a weather prediction based on insect behavior can be than one based on the individualized behavior of humans, or even sows.

If you doubt this consistency in the least, find a black field cricket and get out your stop watch. Crickets are called "the poor man's thermometer" because you can calculate the exact temperature by the speed of their chirps—and with more accuracy than a mercury thermometer, which has both lag and variation. Count the number of chirps the cricket makes during a 15-second interval, then add 37 to the number to get the correct temperature in degrees Fahrenheit. If he chirps 40 times in 15 seconds, the temperature is precisely 77 degrees where the cricket is sitting. And it never varies.

Ants are considered good weather predictors. Theophrastus, writing Greek weather predictions in the fourth century B.C., said, "If ants on the side of a hollow carry their eggs from the nest to the high ground, it indicates rain." And this same statement in slight variations crops up in British and American weather sayings. When ants move en masse during fair weather, their patterns are scattered, but when rain is approaching, all mass movements are made in a single-file line, like a long string of soldiers marching. Ants, sensing approaching rain, will busy themselves building and reinforcing their nests, and when rain is near, the entrances to anthills are closed. This has led to the conclusion that new earth on an anthill means rain, or, as some now-forgotten weather watcher put it:

> If ants their walls do frequent build,
> Rain will from the clouds be spilled.

Spiders are forever hanging around barns and outbuildings, so the farmer has had much occasion to observe this little creature's behavior. When they desert their webs and are seen on walls, it is a sign of bad weather. When they weave their webs, then it means that the weather will improve. And if the spider works on the web during rain, it is only a light shower and will end soon. But the best sign of all is when spiders spin their webs in the morning, as this Japanese saying tells:

> When spiders weave their webs by noon,
> Fine weather is coming soon.

Flying insects, we have already noted when considering the swallows that feed on them, fly lower to the ground just before a storm. Also, the lowering pressure, or perhaps the humidity, irritates many flying insects, such as mosquitoes, flies, and gnats, making them swarm more, cling, and bite more diligently. Thus:

> The gnats bite and I scratch in vain,
> Because they know it is going to rain.

Bees, however, do not swarm before a storm. Just the opposite, bees return to their hives as the humidity increases and do not come back out until after the rain has passed. It is therefore said that a bee's wings never get wet. In weather lore sayings the statement goes:

51

When bees to distance wing their flight
Days are warm and skies are bright;
But when their flight ends near their home,
Stormy weather is sure to come.

or

If bees stay at home, rain will soon come;
If they fly away, fine will be the day.

If the poor man's thermometer is the cricket, it is to the plant world that we must look to find the poor man's barometer. A great number of plants fold up as humidity increases and the rains draw near. Chickweed, wild indigo, tulips, African marigold, clover, convolvulus, and the common lawn-variety dandelion all undergo a closing up of flowers when the rains come, and an unfolding when the sun comes out again. While many plants do the same thing, for some reason the weather watchers throughout history have singled out the pimpernel for recognition:

Pimpernel, pimpernel, tell me true
Whether the weather be fine or no;
No heart can think, no tongue can tell,
The virtues of the pimpernel.

and:

Of pimpernel, whose brilliant flower
Closes against the approaching shower,
Warning the swain to sheltering bower
From humid air secure.

Aratus, *C. L. Prince translation*

Naturally, there are bound to be a few nonconformists to every rule, such as the pitcher plant, which opens its mouth wider before a shower. Mushrooms and toadstools thrive on the high humidity and are seen to come out in abundance just before the dew point is reached. Toadstools appearing in the morning indicate a very damp evening has passed and much rain is expected during the day. Also, moss and seaweed are fine absorbers of moisture, thus the expression holds water:

> Seaweed dry, sunny sky;
> Seaweed wet, rain you'll get.

A number of trees—oak, silver maple, cottonwood, asp, sycamore, poplar, and lime—all give signs of an approaching storm by the leaves curling up, exposing the underside, which is usually a slightly different color. This, however, is such a late sign of a storm that it's like telling someone he's going to fall after you push him out the window. By the time the tree leaves begin to rattle and turn over leaves, the sky itself will be roaring the message that a storm is brewing.

> When leaves show their undersides,
> Be very sure that rain betides.

Animal, vegetable, and, yes, even mineral signs of weather are possible for the weather-wise. For example, stones tell of rain when they sweat. Moisture exudes from stones when the humidity nears the saturation point. This phenomenon, known as "earth sweat," has long been used as an indicator by weather watchers. Brick walls and metal objects also exhibit earth sweat. With metal this leads to some very rapid oxidation, so it is said that if metal rusts overnight, it will rain the next day for sure.

Wood beams and furniture swell with dampness, and, as a result, they tend to creak just before heavy rains. This is seen in Dr. Jenner's *Signs of Rain:* "Hark how the chairs and tables crack!" Also, wood that has been treated with oil normally becomes damp to the feel, and sometimes to the sight, just before a storm. Wooden bowls sweat, and so, to a lesser extent, do porcelain plates as the humidity becomes very high.

Also, the drop in atmospheric pressure before rain can be seen in wells and springs rising higher than usual and sometimes spilling over as the pressure is released. In Kansas they say that a dry well that starts flowing means rain.

In the fires of our earliest ancestors a wealth of weather infor-

mation burned and was soon put to use. Cave men must have realized, for example, that just before a storm fires were harder to
kindle, but once started, burned brighter and warmer. Much later
the blacksmith made use of this fact and waited for stormy days
to do the tasks that required the greatest heat. Burning wood
pops before a storm, and coals become alternately bright and
dim. When lamps were invented, it didn't take long before someone realized that their flame crackled and occasionally flared before a storm, and shortly thereafter another observer noted that
the wicks of lamps and candles developed a fungus growth in
damp weather. Centuries later many of these observations would
be put to verse:

> The nightly virgin while her wheel she plies
> Foresees the storm impending in the skies
> When sparkling lamps their sputtering lights advance,
> And in their sockets oily bubbles dance.

> When in the wearisome, dark, wintry night
> The flickering torches burn with sputtering light,
> Now flaring far and wide, now sinking low,
> While round their wicks the fungus tumours grow;
> When on the hearth the burning ember glows,
> And numerous sparks around the charcoal throws—
> Mark well these signs, though trifling, not in vain,
> Prognostics sure of the impending rain.

> But why abroad to seek prognostics go,
> When ashes vile foretell the falling snow,
> When half consumed the coals to cinders turn,
> And with a sputtering flame the torches burn?
> And hail expect when the burnt cinders white
> With glowing heat send round a glaring light.

Aratus

When there is fire, there is also smoke, and it, too, is an indicator of weather changes. The smoke, actually carbon particles
and mineral ash, is only slightly lighter than air, so when a great

deal of humidity is present in the atmosphere, the smoke becomes moisture ladened and falls. We smokers, then, can at least get the benefit of some weather wisdom from our bad habit. On days when the smoke from a pipe or cigarette hangs in the air for a long time, you can assume a still atmosphere. But if the smoke falls toward the ground, then fully expect rain, as the humidity, along with low pressure, is setting in. Colonials contended that rain showed itself first through the hearth because the soot fell just before a storm and smoke from the chimney didn't want to rise as it should:

> The smoke from chimneys right ascends,
> Then spreading back to earth it bends.

There are hundreds of other indicators that you will learn, some from this book and some from your own experience. They range from guitar strings tightening up and going out of tune to bubbles sitting on soap just before a storm. Some of them, which I am not at all sure are valid, are listed at the end of this chapter to give you some indicators to check out on your own. You will

find, as I have, that many of these bromides that look at first to be pure malarkey have at least a faint element of association to the actual weather. For example, the Negro slaves believed that if you killed a snake and hung it up to dry, it would rain soon. In fact, snakes and other reptiles are out in greater numbers and with heightened activity during low-pressure periods, and therefore there was more chance for the slave to catch and kill a snake. A logical connection between the killing of the snake and a radical weather change, in fact, existed. So, before we dismiss even a seemingly ridiculous weather fable, it is well worth the time to consider why it would have been added to the collective lore. Remember always that everything on this small planet is affected by weather in some way, so everything has the potential to be a weather sign.

A POTPOURRI OF WEATHER SAYINGS

INSECTS AND SPIDERS

Insects flying in numbers just at evening show weather changing to rain.

Ants

Ants that move their eggs and climb,
Rain is coming anytime.

Expect stormy weather when ants travel in lines and fair weather when they scatter.

Ants go into their nests and busy themselves with their eggs before a storm.

An open ant hole indicates clear weather; a closed one, an approaching storm.

Bees

When charged with stormy matter lower the skies,
The busy bee at home her labor plies. . . .

                                                            Aratus

56

Cockroaches

When cockroaches fly, rain will come.

Fireflies

Fireflies fly very low before a rain.

When the glowworm light her lamp,
The air is always damp.

Fleas

When fleas do very many grow,
Then 'twill surely rain or snow.

When eager bites the thirsty flea,
Clouds and rain you sure shall see.

Locusts

The locust sings when it is to be hot and clear.

When locusts are heard, dry weather will follow.

Flies

A fly on your nose you slap and it goes,
If it comes back again, it will bring a good rain.

Wasps

Wasps and hornets biting more eagerly than usual is a sign of rainy weather.

Gnats

If many gnats are seen flying in compact bodies in the beams of the setting sun, there will be fine weather.

Wood lice

If wood lice run about in great numbers, expect rain.

57

Spiders

When tarantulas crawl in the daytime, rain will surely come.

When spiders work at their webs in the morning, expect a fair day.

Spider webs floating at autumn sunset,
Bring a night frost, this you may bet.

Spiders strengthening their webs indicates rain.

If spiders undo their webs, tempests will follow.

When spiders' webs in air do fly
The spell will soon be very dry.

WORMS, REPTILES, AND AMPHIBIANS

Toads

If toads come out of their holes in great numbers, it will rain soon.

Frogs

When frogs warble, they forecast rain.

If frogs make a noise during a cold rain, warm dry weather will follow.

Tree frogs piping during rain indicate that it will continue.

Snakes

When snakes hunt food, rain may be expected; after a rain, they cannot be found.

Snakes and snake trails are often seen near houses and roads before rain.

Worms

If many earthworms appear, rain will follow.

FISH AND OTHER WATER CREATURES

When fish hook well, and when they are hard to haul up, it is a sign of wind.

Cuttlefish

Cuttlefish swimming on the surface presage a storm.

Codfish

When the codfish's eyes are bloated, wind is coming.

The cod is said to take in ballast before a storm.

Trout

When trout refuse bait or fly,
There ever is a storm a-nigh.

Sea Urchins

Sea urchins trying to dig in mud or to cover their bodies with sand foreshadow a storm.

Sharks

Sharks swim out to sea when a wave of cold weather approaches.

Crabs

Before the storm the crab his briny home
Sidelong forsakes, and strives on land to roam.

Eels

If eels are very lively, it is a sign of rain.

They are nought but eels, that never will appear
Till that tempestuous winds or thunder tear
Their slimy beds.

Whales

When porpoises and whales spout about ships at sea,
storms are coming.

Whales "sounding" foretell a storm.

Jellyfish

When many jellyfish appear in the sea, a period of
storms will follow.

Dolphins

Like dolphins when a signal they transmit
To mariners, by arching of the back,
That they to save their ships take counsel fit.

Cockles

Cockles and most shellfish have gravel sticking to their
shells during a storm, which is nature's way to help
weigh them down and protect them from being tossed
around in the surging water.

Snails

When black snails on the road you see,
Then on the morrow rain will be.

BIRDS

Birds on a telephone wire indicate the coming of rain.

If fowls roll in the sand,
Rain is at hand.

When numerous birds their island home forsake,
And to firm land their airy voyage make,
The ploughman, watching their ill-omened flight,
Fears for his golden fields a withering blight.

Aratus

"And generally birds and cocks pecking themselves is a sign of rain; and so when they imitate the sound of water as if it were raining."

Theophrastus

If birds' wings droop, rain is coming.

When a severe cyclone is coming, migrating birds become puzzled, fly in circles, dart, and can be easily decoyed.

Crows

If a crow hollers in the morning, expect rain by night.

Loons

When loons fly out to sea, it will be fine weather; when they fly toward land, it indicates bad weather.

Seagulls

Seagull, seagull, sit on the sand,
It's never good weather while you're on the land.

Larks

Expect fine weather if larks fly high and sing long.

Ravens

If the raven crows, expect rain.

Swans

When swans fly against the wind, rain is coming.

61

Rooks

When rooks sit in rows on dikes and fences, wind is coming.

When rooks fly high, the next day will be fair.

Geese

When the barnyard goose walks south to north,
Rain will surely soon break forth.

The goose and the gander
Begin to meander;
The matter is plain,
They are dancing for rain.

When geese cackle, it will rain.

When tame geese fly, it will rain.

Wild geese, wild geese, ganging to the sea,
Good weather it will be.
Wild geese, wild geese, ganging to the hill,
The weather it will spill.

Morayshire

Cocks

When cocks crow and then drink,
Rain and thunder are on the brink.

If a cock bobs his head after crowing, fair weather will follow.

If the cock crows going to bed,
He will certainly rise with a watery head.

When the rooster crows on the ground,
The rain will fall down;
When he crows on the fence,
The rain will depart hence.

When a cock crows after a shower, clear weather is coming.

Partridges

White partridges (willow grouse) perching high in trees mean a snowstorm is coming.

Spruce partridges (Canada grouse) feeding heavily indicate bad weather.

Herons

If the heron cries in the night as it flies, it means wind.

Heron screeching in the mountains indicates a storm.

Herons flying up and down in the evening, as if not knowing where to rest, means bad weather is approaching.

Swallows

Swallows fly high: clear blue sky;
Swallows fly low: rain we shall know.

Cranes

Expect fair weather when storks and cranes fly high and steady.

Pigeons

If pigeons fly home slowly, it will rain.

Hawks

If the hawk flies into a tree and searches for lice, it is a sign of rain.

Ducks

When ducks quack profusely, they are said to be "calling for rain."

When ducks are driving through the burn,
That night the weather takes a turn.

Martins

Martins fly low before and during rain.

Woodpeckers

When woodpeckers are unusually noisy, rain will come.

Owls

The hooting of the owl is said to foretell rain.

Bluejays

When bluejays call, rain is coming.

Hens

During a shower, if hens run under shelter, it will not last long, but if they stay out, it will be a long storm.

When hens run about acting frightened, a windstorm is coming.

Sparrows

When sparrows perch and fly together in clusters, it will rain.

If sparrows make a lot of noise, rain will follow.

Peacocks

When the peacocke loudly bawls,
Soon we'll have both rain and squalls.

When the peacocke's distant voice you hear,
Are you in want of rain? Rejoice, 'tis almost here.
The proud sun-brewing peacocke with his feathers,
   Walkes all along, thinking himself a king,

And with his voice prognosticates *all* weathers,
  Although, God knows, how badly he doth sing;
But when he looks downe to his base blacke feete,
He droops, and is ashamed of things unmeet.

Chester, Love's Martyr

Guinea Fowls

The calling of Guinea fowls or pea fowls foretell rain.

If when snow is on the ground,
the guinea hens cry, hallow, and caw,
And the turkey moves around,
There will surely be a thaw.

Bluebirds

Bluebirds chatter when it is going to rain.

Starlings

When starlings and crows group together in large numbers, expect rain.

Kingfishers

The peaceful kingfishers are met together
About the decks, and prophesy calm weather.

Robins

If robins enter the barn,
Heavy rains can be expected.

Cuckoos

When the cuckoo sings in the sunny sky,
All the roads will soon be dry.

Turkeys

When water turkeys fly against the wind, rain is coming.

When a turkey stands with his back to the wind so that his feathers become ruffled, a storm is coming.

WILD ANIMALS

Rabbits

When hares seek shelter in the lowlands, snow is on the way.

Rabbits go to the woods before a severe storm.

Bears

Bears and coons are always restless before a storm.

Weasels

When weasels run about in the morning, expect rain later in the day.

Foxes

When foxes bark at night, a storm is on the way.

Moles

When moles throw up earth, rain will follow soon.

When moles throw up earth during a frost, it will thaw within forty-eight hours.

Bats

If bats cry a lot or fly into the house, it will rain.

Wolves

Wolves always howl more before a storm.

When through the dismal night the lone wolf howls,
Or when at eve around the house he prowls,

And, grown familiar, seeks to make his bed,
Careless of man, in some outlying shed,
Then mark: ere thrice Aurora shall arise,
A horrid storm will sweep the blackened skies.

Aratus

Deer

Dear and elk come down from the mountains at least two days before a storm.

Squirrels

When a squirrel eats nuts in a tree,
Weather as warm as warm can be.

Prairie Dogs

Prairie dogs barricade their holes with grass and dirt before a storm.

When prairie dogs are playful, it is a sign of fair weather.

Rats

Rats leave a ship before a storm.

Rats seek protection from the wind on the eve of a storm.

When rats move shavings away from the windward side of a house, it is going to storm.

E'en mice oft-times prophetic are of rain,
Nor did our sires their auguries disdain,
When loudly piping with their voices shrill,
They frolicked, dancing on the downy hill.

Aratus

Rats and mice "bawling" foretell wind.

67

DOMESTICATED ANIMALS
Cattle

When a storm is coming cattle will go under trees if it is to be a shower but will continue to graze if it will be a long rain.

When cattle are on hilltops, fine weather is coming.

When cattle lie down during a light rain, it will pass soon.

When cattle lick their forefeet or scratch themselves more than usual against objects, it will rain.

When cattle stand with their backs to the wind, rain is coming.

When cattle low and gaze at the sky, expect rain.

The herdsmen too, while yet the skies are fair,
Warned by their bullocks, for the storm prepare—
When with rough tongue they lick their polished hoof,
When bellowing loud they seek the sheltering roof,
When form and yoke at close of day released,
On his right side recumbs the wearied beast;
When keenly pluck the goats the oaken bough;
And deeply wallows in the mire and sow.

Aratus

If the bull leads the cows going to pasture, expect rain.

A learned case I now propound,
Pray give an answer as profound;
'Tis why a cow about half an hour
Before there comes a hasty shower
Doth clap her tail against the hedge?

British Apollo

When cows refuse to go to pasture in the morning, it will rain before night.

When cows don't give milk, expect stormy and cold weather.

If cows lie down early in the morning, it will rain before night.

Goats

Goats leave high ground and seek shelter before a storm.

If goats leave their homes during a rain, it will soon clear.

If goats "bawl," it is going to rain.

Pigs

When pigs squeal in winter, there will be a blizzard.

When pigs carry hay or straw in their mouths, there will be rain or wind.

When pigs carry sticks,
The clouds will play tricks;
When they lie in the mud,
No fears of a flood.

Sheep

Before a storm sheep frisk, leap, and butt each other.

When sheep do huddle by tree and bush
Bad weather is coming with wind and slush.

When sheep go to the hills and scatter, expect nice weather.

When sheep or oxen cluster together as if seeking shelter, expect a storm.

Cats

Sailors say that "the cat has a gale of wind in her tail."

When a cat sneezes, it is a sign of rain.

If the cat washes her face over her ear,
'Tis a sign the weather will be fine and clear.

When the cat lies on its brain,
Then it is going to rain.
                Richard Inwards

When cats sit by the fire more than usual or lick their feet, it is a sign of rain.

Good weather may be expected when a cat washes itself, but when it licks its coat against the grain, expect bad weather.

When the cat sits with its tail toward the fire, expect bad weather.

If a cat scratches itself on the fence, expect rain before night.

An old cat frisking about like a kitten foretells a storm.

If the cat's fur looks glossy, it will be pleasant the next day.

If you see sparks when stroking a cat's back, the weather will change soon.

Dogs

When dogs rub themselves in winter, it will thaw soon.

Dogs' tails straighten when rain is near.

When dogs dig holes, howl when anyone goes out, eat grass, or refuse meat, it is a sign of rain.

Sign, too, of rain: his outstretched feet the hound
Extends, and curves his belly to the ground.

A dog rolling on the ground is a sign of violent wind.

Horses

If a horse turns back his lips and grins, it will rain.

Horses foretell rain when they appear restless and uneasy.

Horses race before a wind.

Horses' tails appear larger when rain is coming because the hair is standing erect.

When horses sweat in the stable, it is a sign of rain.

When horses stretch out their necks and sniff the air, it will rain.

Donkeys

When the donkey blows his horn
'Tis time to house your hay and corn.

Mules

If a mule shakes his harness, it will rain soon.

PLANTS

Flowers

When the perfume of flowers is unusually strong, expect rain.

If flowers stay open all night, the weather will be wet the next day.

Trees

When the leaves of trees curl during a south wind, it will rain.

The silver maple shows the lining of its leaves before a storm.

71

Chrysanthemums

There gay chrysanthemums repose,
And when stern tempests lower,
Their silken fringes softly close
Against the shower.

Richard Inwards

Marigolds

The marigold that goes to bed with the sun,
And with him rises, weeping.

Shakespeare, Winter's Tale

Pondweed

Pondweed sinks before a storm.

Pimpernel

Now, look! Our weather-glass is spread—
    The pimpernel, whose flower
Closes its leaves of spotted red
    Against a rainy hour.

Dr. Wilson

Dandelions

When the down of the dandelion closes up, it is a sign
of rain.

Hawkweeds

If the hawkweed closes its flowers in the afternoon, it
will rain.

Chickweed

When chickweed opens its leaves fully, fine weather
will follow; when they close up, expect a storm.

Pitcher Plants

The pitcher plant opens its mouth before rain.

Ferns

When the fern is as high as a ladle,
You may sleep as long as you are able:
When the fern begins to look red,
Then milk is good with brown bread.

Sunflowers

When sunflowers raise their heads, it is a sign of rain.

Clovers

Clover contracts its leaves before a storm.

Trefoils

The stalk of the trefoil swells before rain.

Watercress

If watercress beds steam on a summer evening, the next
day will be hot.

Windflower

The windflower closes its petals and droops before rain.

MISCELLANEOUS

Cream and Milk

When cream and milk turn sour in the night, there are
thunderstorms nearby and they will probably arrive
shortly.

Cream rises to the top of milk most freely with a north
wind.

Ropes

Ropes are more difficult to untwist before bad weather.

Matting

When the matting on the floor shrinks, expect dry weather; when it expands, expect wet weather.

Walls

When walls in cold weather begin to show dampness, the weather will change.

Rivers

A lot of foam on a river foretells a storm.

Doors

Doors and windows are harder to open and shut in damp weather.

Coffee Bubbles

When the bubbles in coffee collect in the center of the cup, the weather will be fair; when they form a ring around the edge of the cup, expect rain; if they float separately over the surface, the weather will be changeable.

Salt

Salt becomes damp before rain.

Pavements

If pavements look rusty, rain may be expected soon.

Stringed Instruments

When stringed instruments give forth clear, ringing sounds, there will be fair weather.

Camphor Gum

Camphor gum will rise in alcohol before rain.

Wells

When water rises in wells and springs, rain is approaching.

Coals

Coals become alternately bright and dim before storms.

If sparks fly when a pot of water is put on the fire, it will rain.

Stones

When stones sweat in the afternoon, it indicates rain.

Kites

If kites fly high, fair weather is coming.

❧

CHAPTER FIVE

In Living Color—The Sky

Aristotle wrote that the violent spectrum of nature's rainbow was precisely the colors that man could not duplicate in pigments, and the modern photographer will admit that the many colors of the sun and sky still elude the filmmaker's science. Man, then and now, stands in awe of the montage of colors emanating from the sun, affixing to them both natural and supernatural meanings. Small wonder, then, that by far the largest collection of weather lore relates to the colors of the sky. And besides being the most universal, they are generally among the most accurate indicators of changes in weather. To quote Virgil's *Georgics:*

> Above the rest, the sun who never lies,
> Foretells the change of weather in the skies.

The colors of the sun are accurate, at least in that they give an honest reading of the moisture content of the atmosphere the rays of light pass through. Light itself, as you probably know, is colorless, but as it passes through the atmosphere and meets up with dust particles and water vapor, the refraction breaks light into the spectrum of violet, blue, green, yellow, and red. Blue is the predominant color of clear daylight skies because it refracts most readily. Yellows and greens designate light passing through dry air. Reds indicate that the sunlight is passing through great quantities of dust. A gray sky means that the atmosphere is heavily laden with water droplets.

Since sunrise and sunset are the times when the multiple colors are seen most often, most color lore is associated with these times. While the colors at dawn and dusk have the same meaning for atmospheric conditions, it must be remembered that they do not have the same effect on us. Weather, remember, moves most often from west to east. The sky reading at sunset, then, is an indication of the next day's weather, since you are looking on the horizon at the western source of that weather. Morning sky signs, conversely, are read as the sun rises in the east. The color of the sky to the east indicates the conditions that have already passed you, and the reading becomes an afterstatement, since the weather you see on the morning horizon is moving away, and your prediction is based on what conditions normally follow after it. While both morning and evening signs are thus significant, the evening signs carry the most certain meaning for the observer and are most often alluded to:

> For oft we find him [sun] finishing his race,
> With various colours erring on his face.
>
> Virgil

Yellow and greens, the short wavelength colors, generally speak of fair weather ahead when viewed at dusk. Yellow, or white-yellow, can be deceptive. Weather lorists say that bright yellow indicates windy, but fair, weather, while a white-yellow sky extending far up is indicative of threatening, stormy weather ahead. Green, however, is a much stronger indicator, though not often seen. The green flash or green ray, if seen as the last color as the sun sinks behind a well-defined horizon, means that the heavens are bone dry and portends of fair weather probably for as long as twenty-four hours.

> Glimpse you e'er the green ray,
> Count the morrow a fine day.

77

Because the green ray is rare, and because it is only a momentary flash of light easily missed entirely, it has also become a part of folk legend. The Scottish Highlanders, for example, say that to see the green ray is to gain powers of seeing into the real feelings of your heart, and thus not to be deceived in matters of love. Regardless of its effect on emotional insights, it's a safe bet that having seen the green ray, the Scotchman could spend the next day courting in the pleasant weather that ensued.

Blue is the color that dominates when there exists a medium concentration of dust and vapor in the atmosphere, and since this is the most common condition by day, skies are most often blue. But when dusk comes, if the skies remain blue or turn purple, then it is an omen of the continuation of fair weather. Thus:

> But if with purple rays he brings the light,
> And a pure heaven resigns to quiet night,
> no rising winds or falling storms are nigh.
>
> Virgil

Red in the evening sky is considered to be an omen of fair weather the next day. This is because the red sky is the result of light passing through high concentrations of dust particles, which, since weather normally travels from west to east, will be overhead tomorrow. But a warning here can save a great deal of confusion for the beginning weather watcher. Most sayings that refer to red actually mean pink. A pink hue is the result of dry dust particles; a deep red sky is the result of moisture-laden dust that is likely to spill as rain. Thus the expression that "a red sun has water in his eye" is true if the hue is actually red. But with evening predictions, the color referred to as "red" is pink, and is an indicator of fair weather approaching. The saying "Red sky at night, sailor's delight," is true, if you remember that in this case the "red" is paler. A better statement of this fact is:

> If the sun goes pale to bed,
> 'Twill rain tomorrow, it is said.

A gray evening sky has virtually no misunderstanding in its statement. It means that the sky is heavy with water droplets that will fall, probably the next day when it reaches you from out of the west.

>Gray evening sky, not one day dry.

Come morning, all the signs which were meaningful the evening before have reversed themselves overnight. Again, this is because in the morning you are looking at a horizon to your east, at weather that has passed you by. Thus a gray horizon at dawn means that the rain clouds have passed, and fair weather should follow. A red sky at dawn means that the red atmosphere has moved on, and chances are that the humidity will be on the rise where you are. Thus:

>If red the sun begin his race,
>Be sure the rain will fall apace.
>In fiery red the sun doth rise,
>Then wades through clouds to mount the skies.

And Shakespeare's *Tempest:*

>A red morn, that ever yet betokened
>Wreck to the seaman, tempest to the field,
> Sorrow to shepherds, woe unto the birds,
>Gust and foul flaws to herdmen and to herds.

While this is, admittedly, not as strong an indicator as an evening sky, the morning light certainly does have some meaning—especially if it is considered with the reading of the evening before. The evening and morning combined prediction concerning red and gray is the most common weather lore statement in virtually every Northern Hemisphere country. A few of them from the United States, Scotland, England, Germany, France, and Italy follow:

>Evening red and morning gray
>Help the traveller on his way;
>Evening gray and morning red
>Bring down rain upon his head.

An evening gray and a morning red
Will send the shepherd wet to bed.
Evening gray and morning red
Make the shepherd hang his head.

Sky red in the morning
Is a sailor's sure warning;
Sky red at night
Is the sailor's delight.

The evening red and the morning gray
Is the sign of a bright and cheery day;
The evening gray and the morning red,
Put on your hat, or you'll wet your head.

Evening red and morning gray
Two sure signs of one fine day.

An evening red and morning gray make the pilgrim sing.

A red evening and a gray morning set the pilgrim a-walking.

Evening red and weather fine,
Morning red, of rain's a sign.

If the evening is red and the morning gray,
It is the sign of a bonnie day;
If the evening's gray and the morning red,
The lamb and the ewe will go wet to bed.

If these brilliant colors appeared in vague forms only, that would certainly be sight enough, but nature stages far grander color-and-light shows for us. As light is scattered by dust, moisture, raindrops, and ice crystals, it produces not only colors, but distinctive patterns. Rainbows, auroras, coronas, halos, St. Elmo's fire, and lightning are the patterns light presents. It is fine entertainment and is of serious meaning for those who would be weather-wise.

The rainbow, called the "bridge to heaven" by the Norsemen, is one of the most brilliant of sights. Its many-hued bands arch

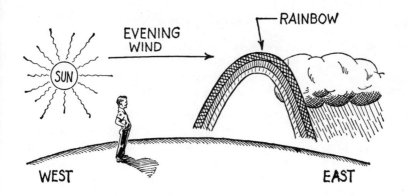

EVENING WIND

RAINBOW

SUN

WEST

EAST

across the sky in morning and late afternoon, virtually demanding attention. For most of us in Western culture, it is considered a sign of good luck to see a rainbow and to speculate about that pot of gold at the end of it. Rainbows are lucky for the weather forecaster, for they are definite statements of change. A rainbow can occur only when rain-heavy clouds are opposite the sun. Obviously, if a rainbow appears before a cloud that is moving toward you, that presages rain. If the rainbow is evident in a cloud moving away from you, that is a sign that the rain clouds have passed and fair weather is to follow. The expression is that if a rainbow appears "in the wind's eye," rain is coming soon. Sailors had another way of putting it:

> Rainbow to windward,
> foul fairs the day.
> Rainbow to leeward,
> damp runs away.

Now we can, as thousands before us have, connect this rainbow logic to our knowledge that in this hemisphere, weather typically moves from the west to the east. The Seneca Indians did this when they said that rainbows in the west bring light showers, and rainbows to the east promise good hunting. The ancient Chinese said of this:

Rainbow in the eastern sky,
the morrow will be dry.
Rainbow in the west that gleams,
rain falls in streams.

Taking this reasoning one step further, we know that rainbows
normally appear in the morning and late afternoon. In the morning the sun is in the eastern sky, and therefore the rainbow will
appear in the west. Now, since the rainbow in the west indicates
a rain cloud coming toward us (a rainbow in the wind's eye),
then it follows that rain is coming. Therefore, a rainbow in the
morning is a relatively accurate statement of rain to come. In the
early evening, the opposite is true. The rainbow appears to us
behind a rain cloud moving eastward, or away, from where we
stand. Therefore, the rainbow in the evening tells of rain past,
and fair weather ahead. Sailors swore by this and looked to rainbows by morning and evening to determine the course of their
day and the cut of their sails. Rainbows, which they called "sun
dogs," thus foretold: "Dog in the morning, sailor, take warning;
dog in the night, a sailor's delight." There were many variations
of this jingle both from the sea and land. A few follow:
from herdsmen:

A rainbow in the morning
Is the shepherd's warning;
A rainbow at night
Is the shepherd's delight.

from farmers:

A rainbow in the morn, put your hook in the corn;
A rainbow at eve, put your head in the sheave.

from sailors:

A weather-gall at morn, fine weather all gone;
A rainbow towards night, fair weather in sight.
Rainbow at night, sailor's delight:
Rainbow in morning, sailors take warning.
Rainbow at noon, rain soon.

The last jingle speaks of a "rainbow at noon." Actually, a rainbow could not be seen at noon because the sun would be directly overhead, and a rainbow could not form. If the expression, however, is taken to mean "middle day," then a rainbow is theoretically possible. And you could see a rainbow at noon from high latitudes. In any event, a noon rainbow would indicate a great deal of moisture at midday, a condition that is conducive to rain.

Another way to summarize the logic of a rainbow's appearance and its meaning is that "if a rainbow appears in fair weather, foul will follow; if a rainbow appears in foul weather, fair will follow." A few moments of reflection of rainbow formation and wind direction will show you why this is generally true.

There is more to a rainbow than just its appearance. The presence in a rainbow of one dominant color is said to have meaning too. If blue is strong, then the air is said to be clearing. Green indicates continued rain. If red shows strong, paling all other colors in comparison, then it is a sign of heavy rains. Also, sailors say rainbows that do not touch the water indicate fair skies. And the American woodsman said that a rainbow coming down the mountainside is a sure sign of storms. How accurate these indicators are is a matter of meteorological speculation, but they do appear to have at least some semblance of meaning and are worthy of consideration.

Coronas, small colored rings around the sun and, in some cases, the stars, also have meaning to weather watchers. The corona is red on the outside and blue on the inner portion of the ring. This color comes from strong light bending through water droplets; thus it indicates rain clouds. But the corona is to be watched carefully, for if it increases or decreases in size, then it will provide yet another indicator. An expanding corona means that the water globules are evaporating and the weather is thus clearing. A shrinking corona means that the water droplets are growing and soon will fall as rain.

Halos are often confused with coronas, since both encircle the sun or moon, but they are much different in origin and meaning. A halo is usually white, occasionally with a red inner ring. It is much larger than a corona, and it does not change in size. Halos are caused by light bending through ice crystals at very high altitudes. These ice crystals are normally present at the top of a major storm center, and are pushed along ahead of the storm, making them a strong indicator of bad weather coming. Thus the words:

> The circle of the sun
> wets the shepherd.

> When the sun is in his house [encircled],
> it will rain soon.

> The moon with a circle
> brings water in her beak.

Or set to verse by Aratus:

> Observe if shorn of circling rays his head,
> And o'er his face a veil of redness spread;
> Far o'er the plains of God of Winds will sweep,
> Lashing the troubled bosom of the deep.

> And foul weather expect, when thou canst trace
> A baleful halo circling Phoebus' face
> Of murky darkness, and approaching near:
> If of two circles, fouler weather fear.
> Mark when from eastern wave his rays emerge,
> And ere he quench them in the western surge,
> If near the horizon ruddy clouds arise,
> Mocking the solar orb in form and size:
> If two such satellites the sun attend,
> Soon will tempestuous rain from heaven descend:
> If one, and north, the northern wind prevails;
> If one, and south, expect the southern gales.

Halos and coronas are most often confused in translating their changing sizes. The corona, remember, grows larger as the water droplets evaporate, and this increase in size indicates clearing weather. The halo does not grow, but it appears to grow and move away as the storm moves it closer to the water and the clouds come down lower. If you don't confuse them, then the following halo indicators are true:

> The bigger the ring,
> the nearer the wet.

and

> When the wheel is far,
> the storm is n'ar.
> When the wheel is n'ar,
> the storm is far.

Aurora borealis, better known as the northern lights, is one of the most awesome displays the heavens present. But it may have the weakest meaning to the weather observer. Two predictions are associated with the appearance of the aurora—thunderstorms and cold weather. To the first, Virgil wrote:

> If Aurora with half-open eyes
> And a pale sickly cheek salutes the skies,
> How shall the vines with tender leaves defend
> Her teeming clusters when the storms descend.

While fine verse, it falls short of defendable weather predicting, since the conditions that bring an aurora are not necessarily those that accompany severe storms. The second, that "northern lights bring cold weather," is also scoffed at by meteorologists. Eric Sloane disagrees with the experts on this point. He notes that cold arctic influxes do accompany the long-range magnetic fields that nurture auroras. It will be left to the careful eye of the weather watcher to resolve this controversy and designate the weather meaning, if any, of aurora borealis.

The meaning of lightning colors is far less controversial. Simply stated, red or yellow lightning will not bring rain, while white lightning (the bolt, not the drink) presages a storm that will reach you. White lightning is seen through clear air, which is typically in the west and headed your way. Red or colored lightning is seen at a distance through dust-packed air, indicative of a storm that will pass to the north or south of your location. Thus the statement:

> Yaller gal, yaller gal, flashing through the night,
> Summer storms will pass you, unless the lightning's white.

The eeriest display of lightning is, of course, St. Elmo's fire. Appearing to be fire without heat or harm, it was often seen on church steeples, on the lances of soldiers, on cows' horns, and, most commonly, flickering across the masts and spars of sailing ships. Shakespeare described this phenomenon in *The Tempest:*

> Sometimes I'd divide
> And burn in many places; on the topmast,
> The yards and bowsprit, would I flame
> distinctly, then meet and join.

Often it is seen dancing on the heads of men, encircling them with a saintlike glow. This may well be the origin of the many saints' names associated with the phenomenon. Besides St. Elmo, St. Helen, St. Telmes, St. Nicholas, and even St. Peter have been linked in name to this strange fire. In some cultures St. Elmo's fire is believed to be a sign of good luck; to mariners it was the ghosts of drowned comrades returning to warn of an approaching storm. Actually, St. Elmo's fire is a simple discharge of the built-up electrical particles in the atmosphere. But since these buildups occur because of a developing storm, they are indeed charged with meaning of foul weather, giving meaning to Longfellow's lines in *The Golden Legend:*

> Last night I saw Saint Elmo's stars,
>   With their glittering lanterns all at play,
> On the tops of the masts and the tips of the spars,
>   And I knew we should have foul weather today.

These, then, are the displays of color and light that provide a source of pleasure along with information about the workings of weather. They are, for the most part, sun signs, since it is the sun's rays that, in bending through the various atmospheric conditions, alter the complexion of the skies and the message. In presenting them, I have attempted to avoid much of the technical explanations, under the assumption that Keats was right when he said, "Philosophy will unweave a rainbow." Still, the light has meaning and challenges us to read. As Virgil said in *Georgics:*

> The sun reveals the secrets of the sky,
> And who dares give the source of light the lie.

87

CHAPTER SIX

ᑲᢊᑭᕊ

Mists in the Heavens—Clouds

Clouds are both the children of weather, and the parents of weather yet to come. The breeding of clouds is attended by temperatures, humidity, and atmospheric conditions that are the determiners of weather, and therefore the clouds themselves tell about coming weather in the shapes, sizes, and heights they develop. Meteorologists call clouds "weather factories" because within many of them conditions develop that create the most tempestuous of offspring. Weather watchers call clouds the "weathermen of the heavens" because they make the most accurate predictions of all.

"And now the mists from earth are clouds in heaven," John Wilson wrote in *The Evening Cloud*, and, in a single memorable line, summarized the formation of clouds. Simply put, water on the earth's surface is heated and evaporates into an invisible mist. The earth's mist rises. To understand why this happens, think of the atmosphere as a pane of glass that magnifies the sun's rays and heats the earth's surface, while the glass itself, the atmosphere, remains cold. The atmosphere is heated, but from the reflected warmth from the earth. Air moves from warm to cold, and therefore, vapor-soaked air moves upward to the cool atmosphere. When the water vapor reaches a level where the air is too cold to hold the vapor, it condenses and forms clouds.

While clouds appear to lead rather sedate lives, they are actually constantly in motion of one kind or another. They grow as the dew point falls and as more moisture is added. They climb higher or lower, depending on the atmosphere and move with the wind at their individual levels, sometimes exactly opposite to surface winds. And they eventually evaporate themselves in the same way that the water on the earth turns to vapor and disappears. In their life cycle the clouds perform the obvious function of spreading life-giving water around the world. They also create weather, which, as you will recall, is partially caused by the uneven heating of the earth's surface. When the sunlight falls on a blanket of clouds, it is reflected back upward, thus the ground area directly below a cloud formation is not warmed

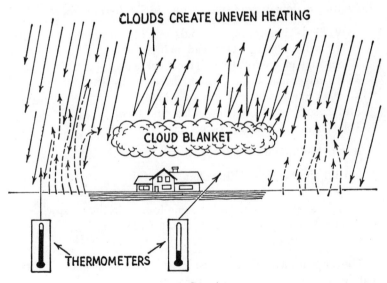

CLOUDS CREATE UNEVEN HEATING

CLOUD BLANKET

THERMOMETERS

nearly as much as the unshaded earth. This creates variations in temperatures that inspire air currents and motions that, in turn, produce variations in the weather.

This cycle is not only thoroughly practical, it is profoundly beautiful. The majestic motion of clouds draws the eye and inspires the pen. Percy Shelley in *The Cloud* wrote as if they were speaking directly, saying:

> I am the daughter of Earth and Water,
> And the nursling of the sky;
> I pass through the pores of the oceans and shores;
> I change, but I cannot die.

Growing clouds, however, are not viewed with as much reverence by the outdoorsman or sailor, who realize that when they begin to multiply or grow, then rains and winds are apt to follow. This is from the obvious fact that since clouds are visible moisture, the more humidity that feeds them, the more clouds, and hence the greater chance of rain. And the more rapid this growth process is, the more severe will be the weather it brings. Thus from Lucretius, a Roman poet, who wrote in *De Rerum Natura:*

> Now clouds combine, and spread o'er all the sky,
> When little rugged parts ascend on high,
> Which may be twined, though by a feeble tie;
> These make small clouds, which, driven on by wind,
> To other like and little clouds are joined,
> And these increase by more: at last they form
> Thick, heavy clouds; and thence proceeds a storm.

and from the Bible (1 Kings 18:44, 45):

> Behold, there ariseth a little cloud out of the
> sea, like a man's hand. . . . Get thee down, that
> the rain stop thee not. And it came to pass in the meanwhile
> that the heaven was black with clouds and wind,
> and there was a great rain.

The appearance of new clouds isn't always negative, fortunately. A few clouds in an otherwise clear sky is even considered a sign of fair weather, so obviously it is the quantity of clouds that makes the determination.

> If on the ocean's bosom clouds appear,
> While the blue vault above is bright and clear,
> These signs by shepherds and by sailors seen,
> Give pleasing hope of days and nights serene.
>
> Aratus

Since a great increase in the number of clouds is a sign of bad weather, it follows that clouds disappearing is a sign of fair weather ahead. And the weather lorists have remembered this by saying that "if you can see enough blue to make a patch for a Dutchman's coat, the weather will clear." This patch phrase has been adopted by many peoples and changed slightly to personalize it. Sailors say "when there is enough blue to make pants for a sailor," while Scotchmen say, to make "a Scot's breeches," and Midwestern Americans say "enough blue to make an old woman's apron," but in all the thought of clearing weather remains the same. Another less known variation is:

> If the sky beyond the clouds is blue,
> Be glad, there is a picnic for you.

Two qualifications of these expressions must be noted in passing. First, the blue patch does mean clearing skies, but it will not improve the weather where you are unless the skies are clearing in the west, which is weather moving toward you. Also, weather watchers are quick to add that even the worst storms have partial breaks or splits, and if they close again, it is said that rain is coming back again soon.

Another generalization about clouds and weather is conditioned on the height at which they form. To understand this you must remember that cloud formation is based on the amount of humidity in the air and the temperature of the surrounding atmosphere. Going back to the bucket image, remember that as atmosphere becomes cooler, it shrinks, or condenses, creating a smaller vessel for moisture. Consequently, a cloud forming very high in the sky means that there was very little humidity, and, therefore, the moisture had to rise very high before condensation could form a visible cloud. This has led to the proverb that:

> The higher the cloud,
> the finer the weather.

The one exception to this truism is the highest clouds of all, the cirrus clouds. As we shall see later, cirrus are not made of the same stuff as other clouds, and they carry a radically different meaning.

Clouds moving higher are fair-weather signs, and clouds coming down mean just the opposite. The lowering of clouds always means an increase in humidity, which is a near-certain indication of rain. And the lower the cloud, the more likely the rains will come, so it is logical that weather lorists say that when a cloud casts a shadow on the earth, it will rain. To cast a shadow, of course, a cloud must be thick and low.

Cloud movement, however, is often unrecognized because the clouds appear to move slowly (an illusion caused by their height) and because there are no reference points in the sky to judge movement alongside of. Mountains solve the second problem by acting as yardsticks that one can use to measure the movement of clouds. The general saying for this is, "When the clouds are upon the hills, they'll come down by the mills." And upon this saying almost every area that has a mountain nearby has developed its own local weather sayings about the clouds coming down, such as:

> When Pembroke puts on his cowl,
>   The Dunion on his hood,
> Then a' the wives of Teviotside,
>   Ken there will be a flood.

———

> When Hall Down has a hat,
> Let Kenton beware of a skat [shower].

———

A cloud on Sidlaw Hills fortells rain to Carmylie.

———

When Falkland Hill puts on his cap,
The Howe o' Fife will get a drap;
And when the Bishop draws his cowl,
Look out for wind and weather foul.

———

When Lookout Mountain has its cap on,
it will rain in two hours.

When a storm of some magnitude is approaching, the winds at
different levels will run in different directions. Usually, the lower-
level clouds will be separated enough so that the observer on the
ground will see clouds moving in two or more directions on different levels at the same time. Weather-wise individuals have
noted for hundreds of years that this is a sure sign a tempest is
brewing overhead. And it was no doubt such a sight that
prompted Shakespeare's line from *King John:* "So foul a sky clears
not without a storm."

The higher clouds moving in a direction different from the surface winds is, according to sailors, an indication that the surface
winds may shift, and if they do, it will be to the direction that
the clouds are moving at the higher level. The high clouds not
only tell of wind direction, but, in one case at least, are said to
point. These pointing clouds are long strips called "salmon clouds"
by sailors and "Noah's ark" by landsmen. When the salmon cloud
points north and south, it is a sign of dry weather coming and
when it points east and west, of storms:

North and south the sign of drought,
East and west the sign of blast.

Also, it is generally true that when a cloud "draws water," it
will rain soon. This illusion of thin lines of water being drawn up
into a cloud was recorded by Aristotle and is actually caused by

the sun behind the cloud sending rays through. The light deflects on the heavy moisture and therefore scatters into narrow beams, which, in the damp air, look like water.

And yet another general rule:

> Sunshine shower won't last half an hour;
> Sunshine shower rain again tomorrow.

Rain that falls while the sun is out and shining is obviously from a very small cloud, yet such little clouds normally don't bring rain unless the air is extremely humid. This is a set of conditions that generally persists with light showers over a two- or three-day stretch.

The color of the clouds, as we discussed in the previous chapter, has much meaning, the most overt being black and white indicators. If you arranged clouds by color from the whitest white to the blackest, you would find that you have also made a scale of rain probability. The lighter the cloud, the less chance it will dump water; the darker the cloud, the more chance of rain. A simple thought, nonetheless recorded in the jingle:

> If clouds be bright,
> 'Twill clear to-night;
> If clouds be dark,
> 'Twill rain, do you hark?

The height of the clouds determines their shape, and the forms clouds take are considered the best indicators of what the heavens have in store for you (weather-wise, that is). The forms are easily distinguished from one another, and since there are but four of them, it should not be difficult to develop recognition of what they are and what they mean.

The highest clouds—up about 20,000 feet or more—are cirrus. Ruskin called them the "drifted wings of many companies of angels," and more down-to-earth weather watchers refer to them as "mares' tails" or "hen scratches." These clouds are made of ice crystals, not the conventional liquid moisture of most clouds. They also travel at great speeds, often exceeding one hundred miles an hour, though their great height makes them appear to move no faster than lower, slower clouds. These are the first signs of a large, slow-moving warm front coming and an indication of the increase in wind and possible rain as the front arrives several hours, or as much as a day, later. As such, the mares' tails have long been watched as the earliest sign of a weather change. The proverbs have it that:

> Mares' tails, mares' tails,
> make lofty ships carry low sails.

and

> Hen scratches and filly tails
> Get ready to reef your top sails.

and

> Trace the sky the painter's brush,
> the winds around you soon will rush.

and

> Clouds look as if scratched by a hen,
> Be ready to reef your top sails in.

The next sign of an approaching warm front comes from the next lower level of clouds moving in—the alto-cumulus. (Remember that a warm front's approach means a gradual lowering of clouds in an inverted wedge shape moving in from the west.) The alto-cumulus clouds are made of water droplets that form at an altitude of around 6,500 feet. They look like a flock of lambs, small, fluffy, and white. But the sailor has long called these formations "mackerel skies," and has said of them:

> Mackerel clouds in sky,
> Expect more wet than dry.

and

> Mackerel scales,
> Furl your sails.

and

A mackerel sky,
Not twenty-four hours day.

Since mares' tails and mackerel skies are two signs of the same coming event and appear fairly close together, one reinforces the other. They have taken on identical meanings to the sailors and to many are considered different shapes of the same kind of cloud. While this is not scientifically correct, it has led to fine weather predictions in the combined sayings:

Mackerel sky and mares' tails,
make lofty ships carry low sails.

and

Mares' tails are mackerel sky,
Never long wet, never long dry.

The last line, "Never long wet, never long dry," refers to the drizzle that accompanies a warm front, often intermittent showers that last for many hours. But before the warm front can bring its promised rain, the next level of clouds must move in. These are the stratus clouds. They come in thin sheets of a rather uniform dull gray color. The weather lorists and meteorologists call their overcast a "leaden sky." It begins at around 6,500 feet and, as the front moves in slowly, lowers to very near the earth's surface. These are the clouds that eventually bring the promised monotonous drizzle of a warm front's activity.

It must be noted here that warm front activity is far from a bad weather sign for most of us. Warm fronts do not, as a rule, kick up much of a fuss when passing, and they do bring light showers that are looked for by the farmers. But weather is not always viewed the same way by people in all situations. Therefore it is well to consider how the source of any weather saying views that particular kind of weather. For example, in India rains are a blessing, since the great fear is of drought, and India's weather lore always depicts storms—even violent ones—as "good weather"

MARES TAILS—
HIGH AND
FEATHERY

MACKEREL SKY—
"A FLOCK
OF PUFFS"

LEADEN SKY—
FLAT AND
DIRTY

CUMULUS—
SEPARATED THEY
MEAN FAIR
WEATHER

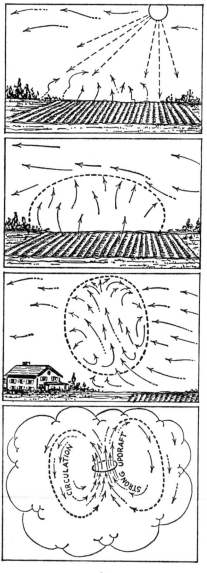

signs. But to the sailor, rain and weather change is almost always cast in negative proverbs because any change from sunny skies and constant winds is troublesome to staying on course and on schedule. Even mariners admit, however, that rain isn't all bad:

> Some rain, some rest;
> Fine weather isn't always best.

When most people think of clouds, they are thinking of the fluffy white cumulus clouds. They appear like large puffs of cotton against a blue sky. When they are few in number and are very white, they are the harbingers of the very best weather—clear, bright, and pleasant. In this form the cumulus clouds never bring rain:

> If woolly fleeces spread the heavenly way,
> Be sure no rain disturbs the summer's day.

But the cumulus clouds are like cuddly-looking lion cubs with all of the potential to grow into the most violent of beasts. To understand this inherent threat, you must realize that a cumulus cloud is actually a ball of very active warm air that meteorologists call a "thermal." Heat forms a bubble on the earth's surface, which is kept from dissipating by higher breezes that form a lid. Eventually the bubble of heat breaks away from earth and becomes a thermal cell rising into the atmosphere. Within the cell the warm air is rising violently upward in the middle, then curling out and down to once again rise in the middle—a process that, if you could see it, would look like a doughnut. Any pilot can tell you that the thermal is very real, as to fly into it is like hitting a bump —the plane jerks suddenly upward and more slowly settles back down. On pleasant days with the very best visibility possible, the thermals are many and make low-altitude flying like driving a car down a rutted side road. As this thermal, or cell of hot air, rises, the dew-point level is finally reached, and the thermal is then visible as a cumulus cloud. The cloud is flat on the bottom, showing where the dew point is, and puffed at the top, which indicates the vertical motion forever at the center of such a cloud.

99

As cumulus clouds become larger and taller, there is more moisture and more vertical upthrusting activity indicated. This looks like the piling up of smaller clouds (though it actually isn't), and weather watchers have long known it as a sign of rain.

> When clouds appear like rocks and towers,
> The earth's refreshed with frequent showers.

And from the Zuni Indians:

> When clouds rise in terraces of white,
> soon will the country of the corn priests
> be pierced with the arrows of rain.

If the cumulus cloud continues to grow, it can develop into the most violent cloud of all, a thundercloud. A thunderstorm is the result of the internal turmoil in a thundercloud, and it can produce hail the size of baseballs, winds strong enough to rip trees from their moorings, and tornadoes with circular winds of 350 miles an hour. The mature thunderstorm cloud can reach up to heights of over 60,000 feet and cover a few miles at its base. The violent updrafts at the center carry water droplets up the center of the cloud. The drops get bigger as they climb, then are dropped down and lifted again until the drops are finally too large for the cloud to hold, and the rain begins. Hail is formed as the water freezes going up in the thunderstorm, but when the pellets fall, the updraft carries them up again, adding more glaze to them with each trip until they, like the water droplets, are too heavy to hold and are literally hurled toward earth. Thus, weather watchers have noted that the raindrops in a thunderstorm are much larger than normal rain, and the size of the drops is an indication of the severity of the storm. As Shakespeare wrote in *The Tempest*:

> And another storm brewing; I hear it sing i' the wind,
> yond' same black cloud, yond' huge one, looks like a
> foul bumbard that would shed his liquor. . . . Yond'
> same cloud cannot chuse but fall by pailfuls.

Finally, all of that internal motion has created a great deal of friction, which, like the friction on the brushes of a dynamo, creates electricity. The lightning bolt is the release of that pent-up friction, and the power of one bolt of lightning is enough to light a city of half a million inhabitants for a month. The thunderstorm, in short, is an awesome display of force.

The thunderstorm is always the product of a cumulus cloud, but the cause of that buildup varies. As we have seen, the earth heating and creating thermals is one source. Moist air blowing up the slopes of mountains can be another cause. But the most common causes are the thunderstorms that occur when an advancing cold front squeezes its way under a warm, moist air mass. A continuous line of individual thunderclouds and storms forms along the front and is called a squall line.

The cumulus cloud, then, becomes a remarkable piece of heavenly hardware. At its best, its snow-white fleece speaks of the fairest weather possible, and at its worst, the thunderstorm can destroy the most stable works of man. It is this paradoxical meaning of the cumulus cloud that was alluded to in the passage:

> And now the mists from earth are clouds in heaven,
> Clouds slowly castellating in a calm
> Sublimer than a storm, while brighter breathes
> O'er the whole firmament the breadth of blue,
> Because of that excessive purity
> Of all those hanging snow-white palaces:
> A gentle contrast, but with power divine.
>
> John Wilson, *Isle of Palms and Other Poems*

CHAPTER SEVEN

ᥫᩤᥬ

Written on the Winds

What causes the wind? The weather. And what brings the weather? Why, the wind, of course. Weather and the winds are inseparably yoked to one another. Wind cannot develop without weather variations, and weather cannot change without wind to move it about. Because of this close relationship, to read the wind correctly is to read the weather. "Every wind has its weather," Bacon said, so all you have to do is understand which weather accompanies which wind direction, speed, duration, at what time of day and under what atmospheric conditions.

To understand the winds you have only to understand how winds are formed and why they go where they go. As we said in Chapter Two, winds are caused by the uneven heating of the earth. Since we live on a sphere, the sun's rays obviously will heat the earth more at the closest point, the equator, and gradually less until we reach its furthest points, the poles. Also, the terrain does not absorb heat at the same rates. Land builds heat faster than water but does not store it as well. Cement-laden cities build heat faster than vegetation-covered countrysides. And since the

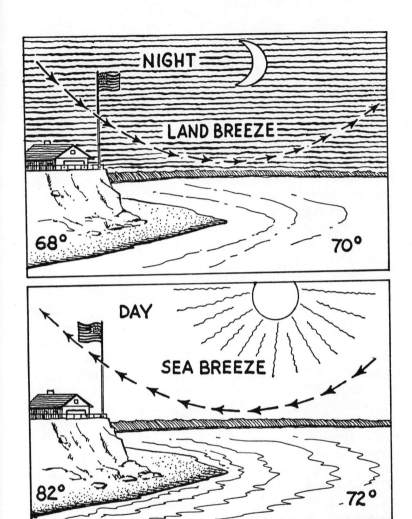

surface varies dramatically from valleys below sea level to mountain peaks thousands of feet above, this, too, causes uneven distances and therefore uneven heating.

Now with all this varied heating, you have only to understand that air moves in an attempt to equalize the temperature and atmospheric pressures (an attempt that is rarely successful). This motion is as often vertical as it is horizontal. The thermals are cases of heated air moving vertically, forming cumulus clouds over the land masses. Sailors have long known this phenomenon and say that if a ship sinks on the open sea, row toward the spot on the horizon where there are clouds, because there will most likely be land underneath them. The simplest example of the uneven heating creating horizontal winds can be seen in coastal breezes. During a summer day the air over the land is warmer than air over the sea, causing a breeze to blow in toward shore, but at night the water is warmer than the land, so the breeze reverses itself and blows out to sea. The mariners remember in saying: "In by day, out by night."

Now comes the point of confusion in realizing that the winds do not move directly in their attempt to equalize heating and pressure. The earth just won't stand still for it. The earth rotates and, in so doing, pushes off a straight course. William Ferrel first defined this law of science in saying, "In whatever direction a body moves on the surface of the earth, there is a force arising from the earth's rotation which deflects it to the right in the Northern Hemisphere and to the left in the Southern Hemisphere." This law applies to many things beyond the winds. The North Atlantic has currents from left to right that sailors have learned to use. Water in the sink will drain in a right-hand motion in the Northern Hemisphere. Rivers cut into their right banks sooner than their left banks. Vines more often climb to the right than the left. If you stand facing north or south and shoot a gun in the Northern Hemisphere, the bullet will veer to the right. And animal watchers say that snakes curl to the right in this hemisphere.

On a global scale, the combination of uneven heating and Ferrel's law on rotation means that major wind patterns, or wind belts, are established moving toward the east in the Northern Hemisphere and toward the west in the Southern Hemisphere. These are the trade winds that sailing ships have depended on for thousands of years.

At two latitudes the pattern does not prevail. The first is called the "doldrums" at the equator. Here, the air currents are all vertical, the air is hot and humid, and there is no wind to bring relief. Further on north and south beyond the trade winds are the horse latitudes, where, again, air motion is vertical. As the tale goes, these latitudes got their name because sailing ships stranded at sea without wind would throw horses overboard in order to save drinking water for the crew during the long wait.

North America, however, is not affected by either the doldrums or by the horse latitudes. The trade-wind pattern of winds from the west toward the east prevail. And on this continent a west wind (out of the west) has been blowing across land surfaces and is therefore generally dry (with the exceptions of the California and Washington State coastlines and western Florida). Therefore, a prevailing west wind is a good sign of mild weather. And folklore here has it that you should do business with a west wind, since men's moods are best in moderate weather.

> When the wind is in the west,
> Suits everyone best.

and

> Wind in the west,
> Weather at its best.

Please note here that this moderately dry west wind is characteristic to most of this continent, but is not universal in its application.

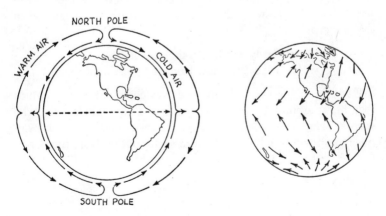

In many parts of the world the prevailing wind most often is moisture laden and brings showers. In the Bible it says, "When ye see a cloud rise out of the west, straightway ye say, there cometh a shower; and so it is." (Luke 12:54.) And it still is, in that particular part of the world.

Also, it should be remembered that weather lorists have not been terribly precise in pinning down the direction of the wind. A west wind means any wind blowing from the west; be it due west or two compass degrees west of north, it's still called a west wind. This has developed because, to the weather watcher, the only difference that counts is one that changes weather, and winds from the west quadrants are quite similar in their meanings on this continent.

A southwest wind has a meaning of its own. These winds are generally warmer and more humid, thus when they go north and are forced to ride up over colder air masses, their temperature falls, and often gentle precipitation results. (The exception to this rule is the Rocky Mountain region.) So the sayings go:

> A wind in the south,
> Has rain in her mouth.

and, from Aristotle (*Problems*):

> 'Tis well to sail
> When the south winds begin to blow.

And since the prevailing wind is from the west, after the south wind blows itself away, the west wind returns as designated in the proverb:

> A southerly wind with showers of rain,
> Will bring the wind from the west again.

Easterly winds are indicative of the counterclockwise winds that blow around low-pressure centers. These winds bring the severest kind of weather in the Northern Hemisphere. This applies to all winds out of the eastern sector, either from the northeast or southeast. In Spain they say that "if it rains with a northeast wind, it rains with a vengeance," and in Ireland they say, "An easterly wind's rain makes fools fain." Zuni Indians recognized that hail came only with storms from the northeast, which they called "winds of the ice fruit." Yankees say:

> When the wind is from the east,
> Neither good for man nor beast.

Repeated throughout the Bible is the evil of an east wind, such as the following passages:

> God prepared a vehement east wind.
>
> Jonah 4:8

> The east wind brought the locust.
>
> Exodus 10:13

> Thou breakest the ships of Tarshish with an east wind.
>
> Psalm 48:7

> The east wind hath broken thee in the midst of the seas.
>
> Ezekiel 27:26

Because of the earth's rotation, wind almost never comes directly from the north. Winds from that direction are fit into either northwest or northeast sayings, and the only thing said about north winds is that they bring cold air. As Shakespeare wrote in *Romeo and Juliet:*

> And more inconstant than the wind, who woos
> Even now the frozen bosom of the north;
> And being angered, puffs away from thence,
> Turning his face to the dew-dropping south.

And there are various combinations of all the wind direction prophecies:

> North winds send hail, south winds bring rain,
> East winds we bewail, west winds blow amain;
> North-east is too cold, south-east not too warm,
> North-west is too bold, south-west doth no harm.

The north is a noyer to grass of all suites,
The east a destroyer to herb and all fruits;
The south, with his showers, refresheth the corn;
The west to all flowers may not be forborne.
The west, as a father, all goodness doth bring;
The east, a forbearer, no manner of thing;
The south, as unkind, draweth sickness too near;
The north, as a friend, maketh all again clear.

Thomas Tusser,
Five Hundred Points of Good Husbandry

and

When the smoke goes west,
Gude weather is past;
When the smoke goes east,
Gude weather comes neist.

and

When the wind south-west
    Under the cloud blows low,
Field-flowers wax their best,
    Fain to be glad and grow.

But when east and by north
    The stark storm strongly blows,
Speedily drives he forth
    All beauty from the rose.

So with a stern needs-be
    The northern blast doth dash
And beat the wide waste sea,
    That it the land may lash.

King Alfred, *Poems*

and from Izaak Walton's *The Compleat Angler:*

When the wind is in the north,
The skillful fisher goes not forth;

108

When the wind is in the east,
'Tis good for neither man nor beast;
When the wind is in the south,
It blows the flies in the fish's mouth;
But when the wind is in the west,
There it is the very best.

How constant are these wind-direction indicators? To answer that, you could travel to Athens and see the Temple of the Winds. Here is a small marble tower fashioned some two thousand years ago. The tower has eight sides, each side with a carving showing a wind direction and the effect of that direction on the weather. The west wind has a figure of a handsome youth with a lapful of flowers. The northeast wind that brings hail is depicted by an old man rattling slingstones in a shield, no doubt to demonstrate the noise of a hailstorm. And the north figure is bundled up, indicating the cold winds that emanate from that sector. The point here is that the wind tower is as accurate an indication of modern Athenian weather now as it was two thousand years ago. The winds have held their course and their meanings.

To obtain even more meaning from the winds, they should be considered in conjunction with the motion of the barometer, which indicates changes in pressure. For the beginning weather watcher, the barometer should be used regularly until the natural indicators of pressure changes can be read from the flights of birds, the motion of insects, the closing of flowers and all of the others. And even when these indicators become second nature to you, the barometer still is helpful both for verification and for heightened precision.

A word of memory refreshment—the barometer's change indicates shifts in pressure. A slowly rising barometer is generally a good weather sign, and a falling barometer a bad weather indicator. The faster the change, the more severe the weather possibilities. High-pressure centers with outward-clockwise winds bring the best weather, while low-pressure centers with inward-counterclockwise winds bring the worst storms. An interesting phenomenon here was discovered by Dr. Buys Ballot in that in this hemisphere if you stand with your back to the wind, the atmospheric pressure will be lower on your left hand than on your right. There are a number of general barometer weather sayings, such as:

> First rise after very low
> Indicates a stormy blow.

and

When the wind backs and the weatherglass [barometer] falls, Then do guard against gales and squalls.

But the chart on the next page is a detailed explanation of which winds and barometric pressure changes indicate coming weather. If you followed it religiously, you would find that for most of this continent it is surprisingly accurate.

Just as a steady barometer indicates continuation of the same weather, a steady wind is a sign of weather stability, too. When winds begin shifting about, they are bringing weather changes. Whirlwinds coming up, for example, are strong storm predictors because they show an unstable atmosphere. Woodsmen say that when the forest whispers, there will be rain soon—the noise coming from gusting winds with downdrafts. And the downdrafts can be seen in smoke from chimneys and pipes that, instead of rising as on a fair day, fall toward the earth.

The veering and backing of winds is an even better prediction tool. A veering wind is one that is changing to a clockwise motion and is a sign of improving weather. A backing wind is a shift to a counterclockwise direction, indicating a low-pressure center and bad weather ahead. To tell whether wind is veering or backing, you can point to where the wind was when the change began, then to where it shifted to, and if the motion of your hand was clockwise, then the wind veered. If your hand motion was counterclockwise, then the wind is backing. So the sayings go:

> A veering wind, fair weather;
> A backing wind, foul weather.

WIND DIRECTION	BAROMETER ACTIVITY	WEATHER RESULTING
east to north	low and falling fast	gales with heavy rains or snowstorms
south to southeast	low and falling fast	severe storm
south to southwest	low and rising	fair weather to follow soon
southwest to northwest	high and steady	continued fair weather
southwest to northwest	falling slowly from high	rain in a day or two
southwest to northwest	extremely high and falling	temperature rising for 24 hours
west	low and rising	clearing and cooler
south to southeast	high and falling fast	high winds and rain within hours
south to southeast	high and falling slow	rain within a day
southeast to northeast	high and falling fast	high winds and rain
southeast to east	high and falling slow	rain within one day
east to northeast	high and falling fast	storms with high winds
east to northeast	high and falling slow	rain in one day
southeast to northeast	low and falling fast	storms and high winds
southeast to northeast	low and falling slow	continuing rains

and

> A veering wind will clear the sky;
> A backing wind says storms are nigh.

And because the westward movement of the sun is a ready reference, these proverbs developed:

> Winds that change against the sun
> Are always sure to backward run.

and

> When the wind veers against the sun,
> Trust it not, for back 'twill run.

and

Winds that swing against the sun,
And winds that bring the rain are one.
Winds that swing round with the sun,
Keep the rainstorm on the run.

Rain sometimes comes before the strong winds, and when this happens, it is a prediction of a real tempest, since the whirling winds of the low-pressure area and the storm itself are giving warning. Thus:

If the rain comes before the wind,
Lower your topsails and take them in;
If the wind comes before the rain,
Lower your topsails and hoist them again.

or:

When wind comes before rain,
Soon you may make sail again.

or:

Wind before a rain,
Set topsails fair again.
Rain before the wind,
Keep topsails snug as sin.

Light winds are not in, and of, themselves much of a weather indicator, and they can often be deceptive, as in the lines from Alexander Ringwood:

Light winds point to pressure low,
But gales around the same do blow.

But strong winds are characteristic of storms, and their arrival is noted:

Blow the wind never so fast,
It will fall at last.

and

Oft is there use of winds that loud
Are whistling o'er the plains;
And oft of heaven-descending rains,
Daughters of the stormy cloud.

Pindar

And as the front approaches, there is a temporary lull, as if to give final warning:

For raging winds blow up incessant showers,
And when the rage allays, the rain begins.

Shakespeare, *Henry IV*

During a rainstorm an increase in the wind speed is a precursor of fair weather to follow. And when the winds blow strongest, they cannot long endure:

The sharper the blast,
The sooner it's past.

And even no wind at all is a weather sign:

No weather is ill,
When winds are still.

As with sky colors and clouds, the evening activity of the wind tells of the next morning's weather. Generally speaking, the winds subside during the evening because at night the earth is not reflecting heat up and stirring the weather-making process. But when the winds continue through the night, they are normally strong and prophesy strong winds and probably rain the next day. At sea the rules do not hold, since, as sailors say, "Winds at night are always bright." But on land the rule is:

The winds of the daytime wrestle and fight
Longer and stronger than those of the night.

and from China:

If wind rises at night
It will fall at daylight.

and from Shakespeare:

> Give not a windy night a rainy morrow.
>
> *Sonnets*

Winds are good natural weather indicators, especially when they are taken into consideration along with changes in pressure, humidity, cloud forms, and the velocity and consistency of the winds themselves. Yet again it is necessary to warn that nothing in nature is absolutely predictable. The Spanish, whose weather lore is rich with wind signs, also show their wisdom with their saying: "When God wills, it rains with any wind."

115

CHAPTER EIGHT

❧

The Dark Side of Forecasting—
Night Signs

After the radiant sunset yields its weather secrets, we are left
beneath a blackened shroud under which cloud, plant, and animal movements fail to provide forecast clues. The night, of
course, offers her own set of weather indicators, but they are
fewer in number and often as subtle and mysterious as the shades
of gray that compose the night itself.

The moon, for example, has long been considered a mysterious
force in nature and an instrument of weather forecasting. The
close heavenly body controls the tides, the rising of sap in trees,
and, according to the Zuni Indians, the affairs of man. This last
point may have some significance, since modern criminologists
tell us there is a correlation between incidence of violent crime
and the full moon. And our Western culture is filled with phrases
linking human behavior to the moon, such as "lunatic" and "moon
struck." Some even believe that the moon affects the severity and
frequency of illness. Thus Shakespeare wrote in *Midsummer
Night's Dream:*

Therefore the moon, the governor of the floods,
Pale in her anger, washes all the air
That rheumatic diseases do abound.

During the eighteenth century, many men of science and medicine believed that the moon was responsible for fevers and a variety of unnamed illnesses. While most of those beliefs have been discounted, some of the observations made of moon influences, when they have been accepted as significant, are of interest. Robert Boyle, for example, was a noted scientist, the creator of Boyle's Law of the Elasticity of Gases, and the founder of the Royal Society. In his work, *Experimenta and Observations Physicae,* he wrote of the moon's influences as follows:

I know an intelligent person, that having, by a very dangerous fall, so broken his head, that divers large pieces of his skull were taken out, as I could easily perceive by the wide scars, that still remain; answered me, that for divers months, that he lay under the chirurgeons hands, he constantly observed, that about full moon, there would be extraordinary prickings and shootings in the wounded parts of his head, as if the meninges were stretched or pressed against the rugged parts of the broken skull; and this with so much pain, as would for two or three nights hinder his sleep, of which at all other times of the moon he used to enjoy a competency. And this gentleman added, that the chirurgeons, (for he had three or four at once) observed from month to month, as well as he, the operation of the full moon upon his head, informing him, that they then manifestly perceived an expansion or intumescence of his brain, which appeared not at all at the new moon. . . .

If the moon is believed to affect the plant and animal worlds, then shouldn't it also have an effect on the weather? That is a question to which weather watchers for thousands of years have given an emphatic "yes" and that modern scientists shrug a shoulder at.

117

For three thousand years the Jewish people have maintained that it never rains on Yom Kippur, the Hebrew Day of Atonement, which always falls in the second week of the lunar month. Midwestern farmers say that timber will splinter if cut during the waning or waxing of the moon. In Germany and England, complete faith was placed in the phases of the moon. They planted by moon phases, washed clothes by them, and even believed moon phases could designate the right time to butcher cattle or take a bride. In the southern Appalachians and in northern Pennsylvania Dutch country, the Old World beliefs in lunar-phase readings continue to this day.

For farmers, the dependency on the moon used to be near absolute, for the obvious reason that the cycles of the moon were more dependable calendars than any that man had devised. The moon became a signpost for planting and led to proverbs of such dubious value as:

> Go plant the beau when the moon is light,
> And yon will find that this is right;
> Plant the potatoes when the moon is dark,
> And to this line you always hark;
> But if you vary from this rule,
> You will find you are a fool;
> If you always follow this rule to the end
> You will always have money to spend.

The mariner has contended for thousands of years that the moon's effect on the tides also has a direct bearing on gales. High tides are said to precede storms at sea and to make the weather more severe. The worst storms are believed to come with "moon tides" or "spring tides," and if the storm continues past ebbing, then it is said to continue for another six hours at minimum. Tide levels are, in fact, associated with weather changes. All storms are related to the changes in atmospheric pressure. The difference in low pressure and high can be as much as a foot difference in water levels in the pressure area of the ocean. Therefore, a close observer can read the ebb and flow of the tides in the same way as other natural barometers are read. And it also follows that a

gale that comes with the tide does do more damage to shore in-
stallations than one with the ebb, by the obvious reason that the
waters will be higher.

Sailors have countless other beliefs in the moon's influence on
weather, some of them summarized in the poem:

> If three days old her face be bright and clear,
> No rain or stormy gale the sailors fear;
> But if she rise with bright and blushing cheek,
> The blustering winds the bending mast will shake.
> If dull her face and blunt her horns appear,
> On the fourth day a breeze or rain is near.
> If on the third she move with horns direct,
> Not pointing downward or to heaven erect,
> The western wind expect; and drenching rain,
> If on the fourth her horns direct remain.
> If to the earth her upper horn she bend,
> Cold Boreas from the north his blast will send;
> If upward she extend it to the sky,
> Loud Notus with his blustering gale is nigh.
> When the fourth day around her orb is spread
> A circling ring of deep and murky red,
> Soon from his cave the God of Storms will rise,
> Dashing with foamy waves the lowering skies,
> And when fair Cynthia her full orb displays,
> Or when unveiled to sight are half her rays,
> Then mark the various hues that paint her face,
> And thus the fickle weather's changes trace.
> If smile her pearly face benign and fair,
> Calm and serene will breathe the balmy air;
> If with deep blush her maiden cheek be red,
> Then boisterous wind the cautious sailors dread;
> If sullen blackness hang upon her brow,
> From clouds as black will rainy torrents flow.
> Not through the month their power these signs extend,
> But all their influence with the quarter end.
>
> Aratus

While a great many of the visible signs read on the face of the moon are completely acceptable weather indicators, the question of whether the lunar phases themselves are of any value to the weather prognosticator remains an area of dispute. (Lunar phases, for those who are not moon gazers, follow a 28/29-day cycle. The New Moon, fully dark faced, begins the phases of waxing, or increasing, up to the Full Moon, then the waning, or darkening, process begins back to the New Moon again.) In 1962 an astronomer at New York University set out to end the arguments. He fed fifty years of U. S. Weather Bureau rainfall data into an IBM computer, along with dates on lunar phases during the same half century. His findings coincided with the sayings of folklore. Rain or snow tends to fall within three days of the new moon with a full 85 per cent probability. At midpoint of waxing or waning, there is a much greater than normal tendency to dryness. Since that experiment, other climatologists have performed similar studies, all producing essentially the same positive results. This would come as no surprise to Theophrastus, who, in the fourth century B.C., wrote that "The ends and beginnings of the lunar months are apt to be stormy." Theophrastus, in fact, believed that the solar and lunar signs were the most important of them all.

MOON PHASES

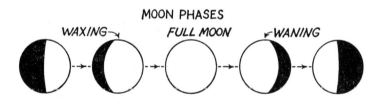

A far less likely lunar-phase prophecy, yet one that has persisted in many Western-culture weather lores is the belief that the fourth, fifth, and sixth days after the new moon somehow foretell what the weather will be like for the remainder of the lunar month. For instance, if these days are dry, then the rest of the lunar month will be dry also. The verses that follow are typical:

As is the fourth and fifth day's weather,
So's that lunation altogether.

and

The first and second never mind,
    The third regard not much;
But as the fourth and fifth you find,
    The rest will be as such.

and

When first the moon appears if then she shrouds
Her silver crescent, tipped with sable clouds,
Conclude she bodes a tempest on the main,
And brews for fields impetuous floods of rain.
Or if her face with fiery flushings glow,
Expect the rattling wind aloft to blow;
But four nights old (for that is the best sign),
With sharpened horns, if glorious then she shines,
Next day not only that, but all the moon,
Till her revolving race be wholly run,
Are void of tempests both by land and sea.

Virgil, *Georgics*

Not content with general prophecies, Sir John Herschel made up a detailed weather chart of his own, based on the time when each phase of the moon begins. In other words, he concluded that if the First Quarter Moon began at 5 A.M. on a summer morning, then rain would follow, but if it began at 2 A.M., then fair weather would be coming. While this has not been scrutinized too closely by modern meteorologists, it does not appear to be too probable. And there is some question as to whether Herschel may have later disowned his chart. Still, almanacs have included the Herschel chart for the better part of a century, and some farmers still refer to it, so it is included on page 123 for your consideration.

Despite the charts, research, and ancient weather sayings on moon phases, the scientific community continues to be highly skeptical of any relationship between the moon and the weather, as attested to by the lines:

> The moon and the weather
>   May change together;
> But change of the moon
>   Does not change the weather.
> If we'd no moon at all,
>   And that may seem strange,
> We still should have weather
>   That's subject to change.

Arthur Machen

Notes and Queries,

September, 1882

Whether you believe the moon causes weather or not, you can nonetheless read its face as a parent reads the facial expressions of a child. Most of the useful clues will come from the complexion and clarity of the moon's features.

With a crescent moon, when the tips, or horns, appear sharp, high winds are a virtual certainty. This is an indication that high-altitude atmosphere is clear, which is nearly always due to high winds aloft. Winds, as discussed in Chapter Seven, tend to work their way down from high altitudes to the surface over a several-hour span. Therefore, sharply defined lines on the face of the moon are good indicators of approaching strong winds. Conversely, if the points, or horns, of the moon appear dull, then you are looking at them through a humid atmosphere, and Virgil's prediction has merit:

> When Luna first her scattered fear recalls,
> If with blunt horns she holds the dusky air,
> Seamen and swains predict abundant showers.

Virgil, *Georgics*

Farmers, always conscious of crop-hurting frosts, know that when the horns of the new moon are clear, or the face of any phase of the moon is clear, then frost is far more likely than on

According to Herschel, if the New Moon, First Quarter Moon, Full Moon or Last Quarter Moon begins during the times listed,* the following weather will result:

IN SUMMER

Time	Forecast
12 to 2 A.M.	Fair
2 to 4 A.M.	Cold and Showers
4 to 6 A.M.	Rain
6 to 10 A.M.	Wind and Rain
10 to noon	Intermittent Showers
noon to 2 P.M.	Heavy rain
2 to 4 P.M.	Changeable
4 to 6 P.M.	Fair
6 to 10 P.M.	Rainy, provided wind is south or southwesterly
10 P.M. to midnight	Fair

IN WINTER

Time	Forecast
12 to 2 A.M.	Frost, unless wind is southwest
2 to 4 A.M.	Snow and Stormy
4 to 6 A.M.	Rain
6 to 8 A.M.	Stormy
8 to 10 A.M.	Cold rain, if wind west
10 to noon	Cold and High Wind
noon to 2 P.M.	Snow and Rain
2 to 4 P.M.	Fair and mild
4 to 6 P.M.	Fair
6 to 8 P.M.	Fair and frosty, if wind is northeast or north
8 to 10 P.M.	Rain or snow, if wind is south or southwest
10 P.M. to midnight	Fair and Frosty

*Note: Lunar-phase times are available both from the U. S. Weather Bureau and from current almanacs.

other nights. This is because on clear nights the cooling of the earth's surface is greatest, and the drop in temperature brings on the condensation on plants we know as frost and dew. Thus the truism:

Clear moon,
Frost soon.

The dulling face of the moon over a several-hour period normally foretells rain. This is a warm front ceiling moving in, changing the features from highly polished to dull, to a complete loss of form as the wedge-shaped air mass approaches. Basing this movement on typical warm front speeds, it is a fairly safe bet that rain will arrive from twelve to fourteen hours after the dulling process begins, or that it will fall about ten hours after the moon loses its visible outline.

A pale moon doth rain.

A halo around the moon, or even more frequently the sun, is probably the best of lunar rain predictors. It precedes rain or snow, and all-around nasty, windy weather. The Scots say, "When 'round the moon there is a broch, the weather will be cold and rough." Checking out this proverb, Rev. C. Swainson spent six years watching for halos in the London skies in the late 1860s. Of 150 halos, virtually all preceded rain within a three-day period. His study seems to indicate that lunar halos foretell rain over a longer period, while solar halos are 80 per cent likely to be followed by rain in less than twenty-four hours. Halos, or half arches around the moon (as with solar halos discussed in Chapter Five), are caused by light traveling through high cirrus ice clouds. And since the cirrus cloud generally is the first sign of an approaching front, and hence possible storms, the moon halos have commonly foretold wet weather:

A moon with a circle brings water in its beak.

and

> Large halo 'round the moon,
> Heavy rains very soon.

and from Longfellow's *Wreck of the Hesperus:*

> For I fear a hurricane;
> Last night the moon had a golden ring,
> And tonight no moon we see.

Mock moons, that is, the illusion of there being more than one moon in the same sky, have the same stormy prediction as halos and for the same reason, that they are seen through cirrus clouds.

> Late, late yestreen I saw the new moon,
> Wi' the old moon in her arms;
> And I fear, I fear, my dear master,
> That we will come to harm.
>
> > *Ballad of Sir Patric Spens*

These mock moons also are frequently found in literature as strange omens of fate, especially if there is more than one mock moon present. Some weather predictors also believe that the more mock moons, the more severe the weather that is predicted. Occasionally as many as six or seven mock moons can be seen, but there is no evidence that a half dozen of them are any more foreboding than one. Also, these mock moons don't move about, so the sighting in the last line from a dialogue in Shakespeare's *King John* must be discounted as a touch of theatrics:

> My lord, they say five moons were seen tonight;
> Four fixed, and the fifth did whirl about
> The other four in wondrous motion.

Have you ever heard the expression "once in a blue moon"? Well, there really is such a moon coloring. It is caused by an atmosphere loaded with volcanic dust or by viewing the moon through clouds that are pink. Either condition is so unusual that the expression "once in a blue moon" has come to mean an exceedingly rare event. The other colors of the moon, however, are not nearly as rare and are far more symptomatic of changing weather. Generally, a silver or white-faced moon indicates a dry atmosphere and fair weather, while a red face means a moist atmosphere and rain coming. So the sayings go:

> If the moon show a silver shield,
> Be not afraid to reap your field;
> But if she rises halved round,
> Soon will tread on deluged ground.

and

> Red moon doth blow;
> White moon neither rain nor snow.

and

> The moon, her face if red be,
> Of water speaks she.
>
> Zuni Indians

and

> If on her cheeks you see the maiden's blush,
> The ruddy moon foreshows that winds will rush.
>
> Virgil, *Georgics*

The stars, like the moon, are weather predictors. Most of the same rules of visibility, or lack of it, that apply to the face of the moon have identical meanings when analyzing the stars. For example, the Maltese say that "the stars twinkle: we cry 'Wind.'" Just as with the horns on the moon, stars twinkle on exceptionally clear nights, indicating strong winds aloft that will probably be surface winds in a matter of hours. Likewise, many stars mean clear visibility and mean there is a greater than normal chance of frost or dew.

> When the stars begin to huddle,
> The earth will soon become a puddle.

This proverb personifies the stars as free spirits capable of going where they wish and even getting together to discuss the weather. Actually, the stars do appear to huddle because the bright stars have halos, and the dimmer stars are totally out of sight—both signs that a thin veil of moisture-laden clouds is dominant.

Finally, if you know your constellations, you may be able to follow the advice in this ancient Greek verse:

> Now mark where high upon the zodiac line
> The stars of lustre-lacking Cancer shine.
> Near to the constellation's southern bound
> Phatne, a nebulous bright spot, is found.
> On either side this cloud, nor distant far,
> Glitters to north and south a little star.
> Though not conspicuous, yet these two are famed—
> The Onoi by ancient sages named.
> If when the sky around be bright and clear,
> Sudden from sight the Phatne disappear,
> And the two Onoi north and south are seen
> Ready to meet—no obstacle between—
> The welkin soon will blacken with rain,
> And torrents rush along the thirsty plain.
> If black the Phatne, and the Onoi clear,
> Sure sign again that drenching showers are near.
> And if the northern star be lost to sight,
> While still the southern glitters fair and bright,
> Notus will blow. But if the southern fail,
> And clearn the northern, Boreas will prevail.
> And as the skies above, the waves below
> Signs of the rising wind and tempest show.
>
> Aratus

On unstable summer nights, so-called "heat lightning" can tell you what the heavens are up to. "Heat lightning" is typically a misnomer. It's actually lightning from a storm in your area. Farmers say, "Summer storms will pass you by unless the lightning's white." A storm headed straight for you is seen through clearer air, so the lightning will seem white. A storm that is bypassing your bailiwick will normally be to the north, south, or east of you, and because it is seen through dirty, still air, the lightning will appear red. Thus, the red, or heat, lightning is no cause to break out the umbrellas.

Each of these night indicators can aid your weather prognosis, but, as this book repeatedly warns, no single clue should be used as the sole basis of your prediction. Just as a doctor doesn't operate on the basis of a single symptom, you shouldn't either. At night, wind direction and barometric pressure ought to be taken into account, along with your natural indicators for a highly probable forecast.

There are actually only two night weather signs that approach 100 per cent dependability. The first is the New England Indian saying that, "When the night has a fever, it cries in the morning." A temperature rise between 9 and 12 P.M. is always followed by rain. The second absolute truth is that if you can't see moon or stars at night, you're standing under a cloud.

CHAPTER NINE

Lore, Legend, and the Litany

Tom Edison had performed thousands of unsuccessful experiments in attempting to develop a storage battery. When asked if he wasn't a bit discouraged, since he had failed so many times, he replied, "What failure? I now know several thousand things that won't work." To develop your own weather wisdom, you will have to emulate Edison in discovering what won't work in order to hit on what will. From the vast body of weather lore, you will have to determine which has meaning for actual "weather" and which is quaint, but discardable, "lore."

That's no mean task, since even the weather experts do not agree on the applicability of much of the lore. Some accept the weather wisdom that animals, birds, reptiles, and plants all anticipate weather changes on a short run; others challenge all or part of these contentions. Some meteorologists argue that sky signs are inconsistent, yet other meteorologists teach these sky shapes and colors and their meanings in classrooms. Some maintain that no weather prediction extending beyond a few hours can be accurate, while others see much grander weather patterns, and a handful of them extend their theories over decades and even centuries to come. Well, as the Bedfordshire poem goes: "Sir, when doctors disagree, who's to decide it, you or me?"

You must decide. You can do it in the same way weather lore was first established, by watching the signs of change in your environment and noting how closely the variables coincide with shifts in weather. Sir John Herschel, one of the leading scientists and philosophers of his time, offered advice on weather lore evaluation along these lines in a treatise *Good Words, the Weather and Weather Reports*. He said:

> . . . any of our readers whose occupations lead them to attend the "signs of the weather," and who from hearing a particular weather adage oft repeated, and from noticing, themselves, marked examples of its verification have begun to put faith in it, to commence keeping a notebook and to set down without bias all the instances which occur to them of the recognized antecedent, and the occurrence or non-occurrence of the expected consequent, not omitting to set down the cases in which it is left undecided—remembering always that the absence of a majority, one way or the other, would, of itself, be an improbability, and that therefore to have any weight, the majority should be a very decided one, and that, not only in itself, but with reference to the neutral instances. We are all involuntarily much more strongly impressed by the fulfillment than by the failure of a prediction, and it is only through thus placing ourselves face to face with fact that we can fully divest ourselves of this bias.

While Herschel's advice is sound, I would pass it along with one caveat—namely, that you have a distinct advantage with the accumulated sayings of thousands of years to start with, and you should not abort this advantage by being too scientifically skeptical at first. A weather saying may appear on the surface to be meaningless or based solely on superstition, yet upon closer examination you may discover some deeper inferences. The situation is not unlike the pure scientist who watched a man drink bourbon and water and become intoxicated. He watched another drink scotch and water and become intoxicated. He watched a third man drink whiskey and water, and he, too, became drunk. From this the scientist reached the conclusion that the water was intoxicating them—since water was the only thing all three drinks had in common. You will have to make a more spirited effort than this scientist and get to the underlying meaning of every weather proverb.

When you do, you will probably find, as I have, that the sky signs are the most dependable, followed closely by insect, bird, wild animal, pet, and finally, your own unsophisticated instincts. But you will also find that even the best weather indicators are not applicable to every region. Every locale has its own distinct weather patterns. You could live five miles from another weather watcher, compare notes, and find a distinct difference in meaning, especially if there happened to be a mountain or a river between you. That means the most accurate predictions are made by people who stay put, such as the farmer who knows that when a certain cloud rises over his neighbor's barn, that means a thunderstorm because he has seen it happen that way many times before. If you are mobile, as much of today's metropolitan population is, then you will have to look for the broader determiners. It can be done; sailors have done it for thousands of years, but not with the same degree of accuracy as the stationary prognosticator.

Some of the meanings of weather lore, you will find, pertain to problems that no longer exist. For example, German farmers said for hundreds of years that hogs should not be slaughtered until after the second frost of winter, and then only when the moon was dark. The dark moon came from the belief, probably unfounded, that the moon produces a chemical that advances spoilage. The second frost, however, was meaningful at the time, since by the time of the second frost, the days would be cool enough to prevent rapid spoiling.

Weather lore is thoroughly inundated with long-range forecasts of all kinds. These, the meteorologists generally say, just can't be so, yet few have checked them out to be sure. Animal predictors are by far the most common here. I avoided presenting these long-range forecasts in the animal-indicator chapter because they are indeed controversial, but they do seem to be worth an honest consideration by supposedly unbiased scientists. In every Western culture people have believed that the thickness of an animal's coat in the fall is a good indicator of the severity of the weather ahead. A thick coat, a cold winter is coming. The skeptics argue that if an animal's fur grows thicker than in other years, that simply means that the previous season has been cooler. True, but one state climatologist who has been studying weather for more than thirty years says there is a continuity in weather—that is, a cooler than usual summer is followed by a colder than usual winter. This would mean that there may, indeed, be some semblance of truth in the collective observations of those who have come before us.

Our ancestors, after all, survived by their ability to cope with nature—without the artificial barriers we have since erected. While they may not always have been right, they were not buffoons either, and their conclusions deserve a thorough hearing. Here are a couple of other animal indicators of seasonal weather that the experts have rejected entirely. I present them to you because I am not so sure they are meaningless. The first dates back to the 1730s; the second is thought to be of both an American Indian and a European origin:

Observe which way the hedgehog builds her nest,
To front the north or south, or east or west;
For it 'tis true what common people say,
The wind will blow the quite contrary way.

and

When the swallow's nest is high
The summer is very dry;
When the swallow buildeth low
You can safely reap and sow.

Many sayings follow this vein of predicting the coming winter by the preparations taken by wild creatures. American Indians taught the white settlers to anticipate the severity of the coming winter by the height and strength of the muskrat house, rabbit's nest, and hornet's nest. It is worth noting here that these beliefs have been thoroughly poo-pooed by the scientific community. Way back in 1883 the matter was put to rest when a scientist, Dr. C. C. Abbott, concluded by his studies that the animals whose autumnal habits were most widely accepted as apocalyptic were most often undependable.

Three more examples of such autumnal predictions should suffice in exploring these oddities. The first indicator is the widely held folk belief that a goose bone will tell how severe the winter will be. This is determined by coloration and size. A row of dark spots on the goose bone is said to be a sure sign of bad winters. And as for size:

> If the November goose bone be thick,
> So will the winter weather be;
> If the November goose bone be thin,
> So will the winter weather be.

The second example is the woolly bear caterpillar, which was long considered as good an indicator as a goose bone, and you didn't even have to cut it up to get your prediction. This caterpillar is black with a brown band around its middle. Pioneers believed that the wider the brown band, the milder the winter would be.

The third example, and my favorite, involves the prognostic ability of the lowly onion. These predictions are generally based on the thickness of the onion skin, but there are numerous variations, including one in which you cut the onion in half on New Year's Eve and, twelve hours later, remove twelve half onion shells and drop a pinch of salt in each (after you've designated which shell represents each of the twelve months). Now, if the salt becomes moist, then that will be a wet month, and if the salt remains dry, you'll be able to predict a dry month. This method certainly is far more complicated, but only slightly more absurd, than the traditional onion saying:

> Onion skins very thin
> Mild winter coming in,
> Onion skins very tough,
> Winter's coming cold and rough.

Such predictions are rather desperate attempts by the farmer to plan crops. He had, and has a critical need to know how the winter will go, and how the next growing season will be. Without this knowledge he is at a loss to know if he should plant corn or wheat, hay or potatoes. Should he cultivate, mulch, or plow deeper than normal? All depends on how the year will go. His most cherished weather proverbs, then, were ones that told him what his growing season would be like. Here are several predictions, all dealing with the same phenomena:

> Year of snow,
> Year of plenty.

and

> March in January,
> January in March.

and

> January wet,
> No wine you get.

and

> January blossoms fill no man's cellar.

and

> Year of snow,
> Fruit will grow.

And Richard Inwards recorded similar sayings from different parts of Europe:

One would rather see a wolf in February
Than a peasant in his shirt sleeves.

Germany

and

A February spring is not worth a pin.

England

and

March flowers make no summer bowers.

France

and

If you see grass in January,
Lock your grain in your granary.

Netherlands

All of these express a belief that the first three months of the year should be cold in order to have a fine growing season. That's a well-founded belief. A cold winter prevents an early thaw and the series of frosts that kill wheat and other crops. Also, a cold winter prevents the fruit trees from blossoming before the frosts which kill them and lead to a barren year. Also, the Bible says that God gives "snow like wool," and the snow blanket, since it is a poor conductor of heat, protects seeds and vegetables into a fine, late spring. Farmers looked for a late spring because they knew it "never deceives."

Along these same lines, the wetness of March is critical. A wet March means that much of the seed will rot in the soil. Thus the sayings:

A bushel of March dust is worth a king's ransom.

and

A wet March,
A sad autumn.

and

135

A bushel of dust in March,
A bushel of silver in September.

and

Thunder in March,
A fruitful harvest.

This last saying gets back to the longing for a cold winter. March seldom has thunderstorm activity, but when it does, it is probably the result of a cold front colliding with a warm front in the area, thus replacing the mild weather with the far more assuring cold March climates.

The farmer also looked to the budding of trees to indicate what the planting season would yield. With a normal growing season the oak tree always buds before the ash. But if the subsoil is drier than normal, then the ash will come out before the oak. Since it also happens that good crops follow the oak's growing pattern more closely than the ash's, the following sayings developed:

If the oak before the ash comes out,
There has been or will be drought.

and

If the oak is out before the ash,
'Twill be a summer of wet and splash;
But if the ash is before the oak,
'Twill be a summer of fire and smoke [drought].

and, the crux of the matter:

If the oak's before the ash,
The farmer's pockets are full of cash.
If the ash is before the oak,
The farmer's hopes will end in smoke.

As a class, meteorologists tend to dismiss long-range forecasts as sheer poppycock. Yet the sayings persist, and for those of us who study them, it is obvious they have a higher degree of accuracy than chance alone would dictate. Admittedly, some of the sayings are patently ridiculous, such as, "a full crop of acorns means a cold winter," and "as high as the weeds grow, just so high will bank the snow," and "the winter can be determined by how far the feathers grow down on the legs of a partridge." But excluding these still leaves many that have merit.

For example, one reason that some seasonal predictions are fairly dependable is that they simply make a statement about the coming season. These predictions are made at the time of the seasonal weather shifts, in the latter parts of March, June, September, and December. These generally coincide with the equinoxes and solstices, which have a decided effect on seasonal weather changes. Thus, when the farmer predicts, "When the wind first blows from the north in November, it will continue to blow from that quarter for three months," he is really only saying that the season has changed, and that during the winter months the prevailing winds are from the northwest instead of west. Hardly profound, but since weather usually develops a little ahead of the seasonal change, such statements are useful weather pattern reminders. And if we agree, at least in principle, that one season's weather sets a pattern for the next, then some of these predictions may well be based on a continuity of nature. Certainly Sir Francis Bacon saw a pattern to nature when he wrote the following prognosis in *De Sapientia Veterum:*

> A severe autumn denotes a windy summer;
> A windy winter a rainy spring;
> A rainy spring a severe summer;
> A severe summer a windy autumn;
> So that the air in balance is
> Seldom debtor unto itself.

If such long-term predictions get only scant attention by serious meteorologists, then those based on ecclesiastical days are rarely noticed at all. After all, isn't this mysticism, spiritualism, and the very quintessence of folklore? The sayings that wind on St. Stephen's Day (September 26) will ruin the grape harvest the next year, or that if it rains on St. Anne's Day (August 26), it will rain for a month and a week, clearly are superstitions based on the lives of saints and the beliefs that developed around them. These are attempts, not to determine cause-and-effect relationships to weather, but to set some higher meaning to the order of natural events.

Again, this reasoning applies generally enough to ecclesiastical predictions, but it does not explain all of them. Some of these saint's day predictions are little more than statements of fact about what the weather usually is on that day. For example, in England they say St. Margaret's Day is always wet and refer to it as "Margaret's Flood." St. Margaret's Day falls on August 20, a date in England which is historically rainy, making Margaret's Flood a reality more often than not. Other saint's day predictions state equally unmystic facts, such as "On St. Patrick's Day (March 17) the warm side of a stone turns up (meaning the snows melt), and the goose begins to lay. Others give advice to husbandrymen, such as, "He who shears his sheep on St. Servatius' Day (May 13) loves his wool more than his sheep."

Many of these seemingly religious predictions have as little relation to the holy day itself as Santa Claus has to the birth of Christ. They simply were formulated at a time when every child in the Western world knew the dates of the saints' days as well as he knew his own birth date. So the saints' days simply became signposts of the year. For proof of this, one has only to read a few letters written by almost anyone in Europe over the past five hundred years and see how the saints' days were used as a calendar: "Plan to visit around St. Chad's . . ." or "It was on Jude's Day last when . . ." When asked about seasonal changes a couple of hundred years back, you would probably have been told that spring begins on St. Peter's Day (February 22), summer starts on St. Urban's Day (May 25), fall takes over on St. Bartholomew's Day (August 24), and the winter is ushered in by St. Clement's Day (November 23). While these were the days when seasons officially arrived, weather predictions were typically made on the saints' days preceding them. Thus, spring predictions were more often based on Candlemas Day (February 2) than on St. Peter's Day.

The only real shortcoming to such a spiritual calendar was that belief in the prediction became dogmatized, and to question the lore was at times tantamount to attacking the religious order. It was this yoking of weather lore with Catholicism that prompted the iconoclastic Henry VIII of England to ban all almanacs with saints' days predictions during his reign. And it is this yoking of the temporal and spiritual that makes it difficult for you and me to separate the weather wisdoms from the weather litany of the time. But the effort can be rewarding, so at the end of this chapter I have included a listing of most of the saints' days and what they are purported to mean to weather watchers.

Being more Protestant than Catholic and more pragmatic than pious, Americans dropped most of the saints' days they had brought with them from Europe. There are, however, two exceptions worth considering. One is the Yankeeization of Candlemas Day, and the other is the continued belief in the weather meaning of Christmas.

Candlemas Day (February 2nd) began in the early days of Catholicism as the feast of the purification of Mary. It falls at the beginning of February, a month farmers have believed for thousands of years to be a "weather breeder," a period of change in which future weather patterns are set. A cold February is vital, farmers believe, for a good crop, and therefore this time around Candlemas was watched with great anticipation. A few of the many weather predictions based on Candlemas Day follow:

> If Candlemas Day be fine and clear,
> We shall have winter half the year.

> If Candlemas Day be mild and gay,
> Go saddle your horses and buy them hay,
> If Candlemas Day be stormy and black,
> It carries the winter away on its back.

139

When it rains on Candlemas Day, the cold is done.

———

Just so far as the sun shines in on Candlemas Day,
Just so far will the snow blow in before May.

———

Half your wood and half your hay,
Should be remaining on Candlemas Day.

———

The shepherd would rather see the wolf enter his flock
Than see the sun on Candlemas Day.

———

Foul weather is no news;
Hail, rain and snow
Are now expected, and
Esteemed no woe:
Nay, 'tis an omen bad,
The yeomen say,
If Phoebus shows his face
The second day.

> *Country Almanack,* 1676

Now when Candlemas Day migrated to the New World, it was
varied slightly at first, such as the Massachusetts saying:

> If Candlemas Day is fair and bright,
> Winter will take another fight:
> If Candlemas Day bring storm and rain,
> Winter is gone and will not come again.

About this time the Pennsylvania Protestants were adapting
their own Germanic lore to their adopted land. In Germany there
is a belief that if the woodchuck sees the sun and is enticed to
come out on Candlemas Day, he will see his shadow and go back

in for four to six weeks more. In France, this same tradition is based on the bear, who not only has to see his shadow, but has to turn around three times, then go back in. In Pennsylvania, the groundhog became the weather bearer for Candlemas Day, and the term of his incarceration, should he see his shadow, was set at six weeks. It is fascinating to watch the evolution of such a weather saying, in this case, one that started around the feast of the Virgin Mary, and degenerated to a groundhog afraid of its own shadow.

The second set of Christian holiday prophecies that was accepted in America pertains to the birth of Christ. The predictions are many and varied, but most assume that the weather during the twelve days of Christmas is prophetic of the weather during the following twelve months, or, as the eastern settlers put it: "The twelve days of Christmas make the almanac for the year." A variation of the twelve-day theme tends more toward the belief that there are critical periods that do breed weather and, hence, will deliver after a specified gestation time. Here are a few of the more common ones:

A warm Christmas,
a cold Easter.

If ice will bear a man at Christmas,
It will not bear a mouse afterward.

A green Christmas, a white Easter.

If the sun shines through the apple tree on Christmas
Day, the following year will have an abundant harvest.

If at Christmas ice hangs on the trees,
Clover may be cut at Easter.

If on Christmas night wine ferments in the barrel,
a good wine year will follow.

———

If windy on Christmas,
Trees will bring much fruit.

———

A green Christmas makes a fat churchyard.

And finally, the longest and most all-encompassing of the lot, taken from a set of poems in the British Museum and first located and printed in *Weather Proverbs,* by W. J. Humphreys:

> Lordlings, all of you I warn:
> If the day that Christ was born
> Fall upon a Sunday,
> The winter shall be good I say,
> But great winds aloft shall be;
> The summer shall be fair and dry.
> By kind skill and without loss,
> Through all lands there shall be peace,
> Good time for all things to be done,
> But he that stealeth shall be found soon;
> What child that day born may be,
> A great lord he shall live to be.
>
> If Christmas day on Monday be,
> A great winter that year you'll see,
> And full of winds, both loud and shrill,
> But in the summer, truth to tell,
> Stern winds shall there be and strong,
> Full of tempests lasting long;
> While battles they shall multiply,
> And great plenty of beasts shall die.
> They that be born that day I mean,
> They shall be strong each one and keen.

He shall be found that stealeth ought,
Though thou be sick thou dieth not.

If Christmas day on Tuesday be,
That year shall many women die,
And that winter grow great marvels;
Ships shall be in great perils.
That year shall kings and lords be slain,
And many other people near them;
A dry summer that year shall be,
As all that are born therein may see;
They shall be strong and covetous.
If thou steal aught, thou losest thy life,
For thou shalt die through sword or knife
But if thou fall sick 'tis certain
Thou shalt turn to life again.

If Christmas day, the truth to say,
Fall upon a Wednesday,
There shall be a hard winter and strong,
With many hideous winds among.
The summer merry and good shall be,
And that year wheat in great plenty;
Young folks shall die that year, also,
And ships at sea shall have great woe.
Whatever child that day born is,
He shall be doughty and gay, I wis,
And wise and crafty also of deed,
And find many in clothes and bread.

If Christmas day on Thursday be
A windy winter you shall see;
Windy weather in each week,
And hard tempests strong and thick.
The summer shall be good and dry,
Corn and beasts shall multiply;
That year is good lands for to till;
Kings and princes shall die by skill,

If a child that day born should be,
It shall happen right well for thee;
Of deeds he shall be good and stable,
Wise of speech and reasonable,
Whoso that day goes thieving about,
He shall be punished without doubt;
And if sickness that day betide
It shall quickly from thee glide.

If Christmas day on Friday be,
The first of winter hard shall be;
With frost and snow, and with great flood,
But the end thereof it shall be good.
Again, the summer shall be good also;
Folk in their eyes shall have great woe;
Women with child, beasts, and corn,
Shall multiply and be lost none.
The child that is born on that day,
Shall live long and lecherous be alway.
Who stealeth ought shall be found out;
If thou be sick it lasteth not.

If Christmas day on Saturday fall,
That winter's to be dreaded by all;
It shall be so full of great tempest,
That it shall slay both man and beast;
Great store shall fail of fruit and corn,
And old fold die many a one.
What woman that day of child doth travail,
She shall give birth in great peril;
And children born that day be faith,
In half a year shall meet with death.
The summer shall be wet and ill;
Thou shalt suffer if aught thou steal;
Thou diest of sickness do thee take.

Well worth considering in evaluating even the more believable
ecclesiastical weather signs is that they no longer pertain to the

actual day for which the prediction was made. The calendars, once inaccurate, have been updated since these sayings were first pronounced during the early Christian Era. In 1752, for example, King George II changed the calendar, tossing out eleven days in September. While these calendar changes were usually performed to bring them more in line with the true celestial year, they nonetheless interject another point of inaccuracy into the weather predictions based on prechange dates.

But if you're attuned to believing in the mystical aspects of weather, then it is only a short step to casting your lot with the believers in weather witchcraft. Beliefs in warlocks and witches who could raise storms and swarm locusts was prevalent well into the nineteenth century, and there is new-found interest in the subject among modern cultists. For these early peoples such beliefs seem reasonable enough. There were two forces in the universe, God and Satan, and both could have an immediate and profound impact on man's existence. Horace Beck, in *Folklore and the Sea*, gives numerous examples of witches brewing up storms and the incantations used by sailors to ward them off. Beck notes that sailors carried knives of cold steel with the handles shaped into a crucifix to ward off the devil, and in calms the sailor had only to "scratch the mast and whistle" to break the stillness.

While the black arts strain the imagination, weather predictions based on the days of the week, month, or year are certain to give logical thinkers mental hernias. Here are samplings of these predictions:

The month that comes in good, goes out bad.

———

The first three days of any season
rule the weather for that season.

———

Clearing on Wednesday,
Clear 'til Sunday.

———

A wet Sunday,
A fine Monday.

———

Never a Saturday without some sunshine.

———

Right as the Friday, soothly for to telle,
Now it shyneth, now it reyneth faste,
Right so can gery Venus overcaste
The hertes of his folk; right as hir day
Is gerful, right so chaungeth she array;
Selde is the Friday al the wyke y-lyke.

Chaucer, *Canterbury Tales*

You can delight in all of the weather sayings that turn the tables and make a prediction of human events based on weather, such as, "If it rains on the day you are wed, it is a sign many tears will be shed." And for those who go further in soothsaying, an old almanac verse goes:

Married in January's chilling time,
Widowed you'll be before your prime.
  Married in February's sleety weather,
  Life you'll tread in tune together.
Married when March winds shrill and roar,
Your home will be on a foreign shore.
  Married 'neath April's changeful skies,
  A checkered path before you lies.

146

Married when bees over May blossoms flit,
Strangers around your board will sit.
　Married in merry month of June,
　Life will be one honeymoon.
Married as July's flower banks blaze,
Bitter-sweet memories in after days.
　Married in August heat and drowse,
　Lover and friend in your chosen spouse.
Married in gold September glow,
Smooth and serene your life will flow.
　Married when leaves in October thin,
　Toil and hardships for you begin.
Married in veils of November mist,
Fortune your wedding ring has missed.
　Married in days of December cheer,
　Love will shine brighter year after year.

What has all this to do with weather wisdom? Well, if little
else, it can serve as bad examples. But it can also aid our understanding of the people who came before us. To watch the evolution of proverbs, such as those we saw develop around Candlemas
Day, certainly can hold a fascination for us. In such evolutions
weather sayings become part of our heritage—American artifacts
as meaningful as a weather vane on a Kansas barn or a hex sign
on a barn in Pennsylvania. While the accuracy of most of these
sayings must crumple by the weight of their own demerit, the
sayings themselves can have value to us even in failure.

SAINTS' DAYS WEATHER CALENDAR

JANUARY

St. Hilary (14)	Said to be the coldest day of the year.
St. Sulpicius (17)	Frost on this day means a good spring in France.
St. Vincent (22)	Sun on this day means good wine crops next season.

147

St. Paul (25)

If St. Paul's be fair and clear,
It promises a happy year;
But if it chances to snow or rain,
There will be dear all sorts of grain;
Or if the wind does blow aloft,
Great stirs will vex the world full oft.

FEBRUARY

St. Bridget (1)

Snow on this day indicates full ditches come spring.

Candlemas Day (2)

A clear, bright day means a late spring.

St. Dorothea (6)

She brings the most snow.

St. Eulalie (12)

If the sun does smile on St. Eulalie's Day, Good for apples and cider, they say.

St. Valentine (14)

Spring is a near neighbor.

St. Peter (22)

The night of this day indicates the weather for the next forty days.

St. Matthias (24)

If there is ice it will break it;
If no ice, it will make it.

St. Romanus (28)

St. Romanus bright and clear,
Augurs a goodly year.

MARCH

St. David (1)

On St. David's Day
Put oats and barley in the clay.

St. Winwaloe (3)

Winwaloe comes as if he were mad (tempestuous).

St. Patrick (17)

The warm side of a stone turns up,
and the broad-back goose begins to lay.

St. Joseph (19)

St. Joseph's day clear,
So follows a fertile year.

St. Benoit (21)   If it rains this day, it will rain for forty days.

The Annunciation (25)   A clear St. Mary's Day, a fruitful year ahead.

APRIL

St. Vincent (5)   If this day is fair, there will be more water than wine.

St. George (23)   If by this time the rye has grown high enough to hide a crow, a good harvest can be expected.

St. Mark (25)   Rain on this day speaks ill for fruit crops.

MAY

St. Jacob (1)   Rain on Jacob's Day, expect a fertile year.

St. Pancras (12)   Does not pass without frost.

St. Servatius (13)   He who shears his sheep before St. Servatius loves more his wool than his sheep.

St. Urban (25)   Once considered the inauguration of summer.

St. Philip (26)   If it rains on St. Philip's Day, the poor will not need help from the rich.

JUNE

St. Barnabas (11)   Rain on Barnabas is good for grapes.

St. Vitus (15)   If St. Vitus' Day be rainy weather, It will rain for thirty days together.

Poor Robin's Almanac, 1697

149

St. John's *Eve* (23)	If it rains on St. John's Eve, the filberts (nuts) will be spoiled.
St. John (24)	No crop before St. John's Day is worthy of praising.

JULY

St. Mary (2)	If it rains on this day, it will rain for a month straight.
St. Martin Bullion (4)	If Martin Bullion's Day brings rain, it will rain for forty days and nights.
St. Gallo (15)	The weather on this day will last for forty days.
St. Swithin (15)	St. Swithin's Day, if ye do rain, For forty days it will remain.
St. Jacob (25)	Puffy white clouds (cumulus) on this day foretells much snow in the coming winter.
St. Anne (26)	Rain on St. Anne's will continue for a month and a week.
St. Godelieve (27)	Rain on this day will continue for forty days.

AUGUST

St. Lawrence (10)	Fine weather on this day indicates a good autumn.
St. Margaret (22)	"Margaret's Flood"; expect rain.
St. Bartholomew (24)	Bartholomew brings dew.

SEPTEMBER

St. Matthew (2)	Matthew's Day bright and clear Brings good wine in next year.

St. Michael (29)	As many days old as the moon is on Michaelmas, so many floods after.

OCTOBER

St. Gallus (16)	No rain on Gallus, a dry spring will follow.
St. Luke (18)	"St. Luke's Little Summer" is the term used for the pleasant (Indian summer-like) weather at this time of year.
St. Simon (28)	St. Simon's is never dry.

NOVEMBER

All Saints' Day (1)	If the beech acorn is wet on this day, so will the winter be wet.
St. Martin (11)	If St. Martin's Day is dry and cold, the winter will not be long lasting.

DECEMBER

Christmas (25)	Foretells the coming year.
St. Stephen (26)	Wind on St. Stephen's Day foretells of bad grapes the following year.
Innocents' Day (28)	A bright day, a year of plenty; A dark, wet day, a year of scarcity.

RELIGIOUS HOLIDAYS WITH VARYING DATES

Shrove Tuesday	When the sun is shining on Shrove Tuesday, It means well for rye and peas.
Ash Wednesday	The wind that prevails on this day will remain throughout Lent.
Lent	Dry Lent, fertile year.

Palm Sunday	A bad Palm Sunday denotes a year of failing crops. (Also, the wind direction on this day is said to dominate throughout the summer.)
Good Friday	A wet Good Friday, very little hay.
Easter	The weather on this day is supposed to indicate the weather at harvest time. Also, pleasant Easter weather means a bountiful crop and harvest.
Paster Sunday	Rain on Paster Sunday means rain on every Sunday until Pentecost.
Pentecost (also Whit-sunday)	Rain on Pentecost forebodes evil.
Corpus Christi	Corpus Christi Day clear, Gives a good year.
All Fools' Day	If it thunders on All Fools' Day, 'Twill bring good crops of corn and hay.

CHAPTER TEN

ᥴ᷈ᢳᢳᥱ

Weather Lore—Past and Prologue

"Past is prologue," Shakespeare said, and any attempt to gain weather wisdom must delve deeply into the accumulated wealth of Western literature. As you may have noted in reading the many poetic stanzas on weather in this book, our literary heritage is thoroughly inundated with insights into nature's moods.

To ferret out weather wisdoms by going back four thousand years to the writings of Aristotle, Theophrastus, and Aratus isn't really necessary. You need not even read all of the literature of Western civilization to capture weather lines from Virgil, Chaucer, Shakespeare, or Shelley. For most of these insights have been gleaned for us in a remarkable series of books and articles written in the past century. In this final chapter, I would like to introduce some of that literature to you so that your search for weather wisdom need not stop when this book is relegated to a bookshelf.

Interest in compiling the weather insights of our culture came about in the mid-nineteenth century, largely due to the work of a single Englishman, Richard Inwards. Like Herschel and other

Renaissance men of his day, Inwards took an active interest in all of the sciences and arts. He was an inventor, a painter, and sculptor, an astronomer, explorer, and meteorologist. He had the advantage of being a friend of John Ruskin, who himself was interested in meteorology, plus Inwards had the good fortune to be born in Bedfordshire, a town rich in its own weather folklore. Inwards, no doubt impressed by a small book produced by the Percy Society entitled *A Collection of Proverbs and Popular Sayings,* set out to develop a comprehensive collection of British weather lore of his own. In 1869 Inwards published the first edition of *Weather Lore.* It was immensely popular, and Inwards worked for the next quarter century to add to it and in 1893 printed the second edition of 200 pages and finally in 1898 his third edition with 245 pages of weather lore. The thousands of weather sayings in Inwards' book are presented without analysis or comment. It is merely a compilation, but the most extensive one to date on British weather. Inwards' *Weather Lore* has gone through many printings, the latest of which is 1969 by Rider and Company. Since most English weather sayings are as applicable to the rocky shores of Maine as they are to the cliffs of Dover, Inwards' book is must reading for all those interested in this art.

In the same ilk is Rev. C. Swainson's *Handbook of Weather Folklore,* first printed in 1873. Rev. Swainson endeavored to expand on the work of Inwards by including all of the folk sayings from the Continent as well. His work contains weather proverbs from Germany, Italy, France, and Greece. Unfortunately, Swainson retained the native languages of each, so unless you are polylinguistic or are willing to bear the expense of translation, the Swainson book will present an obstacle to you.

In America it took an army of men to do what Inwards had done alone in England. The U. S. Army produced the first real collection of Yankee weather lore. It was in 1881 that Major General W. B. Hazen, Chief Signal Officer of the U. S. Army, issued an order to all Army post commanders that they were to collect all "popular weather proverbs and prognostics." Not content with a vague request, General Hazen specified twenty-four overall categories in which the Army was to collect weather sayings, and in his directive he broke the listings down still further so that it included all of the proverbs relating to: sun, moon, stars, meteors, rainbows, mist, fog, dew, clouds, frost, snow, rain, thunder, lightning, and winds. From the living sector he asked for sayings on: animals, birds, fish, reptiles, insects, trees, and all of the inanimate objects, such as furniture, fireplaces, ditches, doors, dust, salt, seed, smoke, soap, strings, and walls. Then he added another category of sayings related to the days of the week, months, seasons, years, and finally, a catchall miscellaneous category.

As is the norm in the Army, the task of compiling all of this raw lore fell down the ranks to a Lieutenant H. H. C. Dunwoody, a signal officer in the Fourth Artillery. Lieutenant Dunwoody did an excellent job in organizing the American weather lore, and, unlike Inwards, he made comments of his own from time to time throughout the collection. Dunwoody's collection was published as *U. S. Army Signal Service Notes Number IX,* by the Government Printing Office in 1883. Copies of this book are widely available in major libraries and, perhaps even more than Inwards, should be read to get a feel for the Yankee variations of weather lore.

Dunwoody's work was followed by another lengthy collection made by Professor of Meteorology Edward Garriott and published by the youthful U. S. Weather Bureau, which, when the collection appeared in 1903, was part of the U. S. Department of Agriculture. The first major collection of weather sayings not underwritten by government was *Weather Proverbs and Paradoxes,* published in 1923 by a meteorological physicist, William J. Humphreys. His book is both well organized and thoroughly enlightening.

While a variety of books have devoted a line, a paragraph, or even as much as a chapter to these folk wisdoms, only one man has given the subject any serious consideration over the last two decades. He is Eric Sloane. A Connecticut Yankee, Eric Sloane combines his insights as a sailor, pilot, and weather historian into a number of excellent books on the weather sciences. Most of his fact books are laced with folksy anecdotes and proverbs, but one small volume, *Folklore of American Weather,* is completely devoted to the subject and, I believe, is as aesthetic as it is insightful.

With the exception of Sloane's books, all of these anthologies of weather lore merely record the sayings without comment on the culture of the people who lived by them. To me this is a lot like eating a synthetic steak—the nourishment is present, but the flavor is missing. To get the flavor of weather folklore I believe you should spend some time reading almanacs.

Almanacs have been the central depository of weather observations since their inception in Egypt around 3000 B.C. Literally, "almanac" is an Arabic word that means "calendar of the skies," and throughout the centuries they have remained faithful to this definition, giving movements of planets, stars, the moon, and predictions of eclipses. As did the astrologers, the ancient almanac

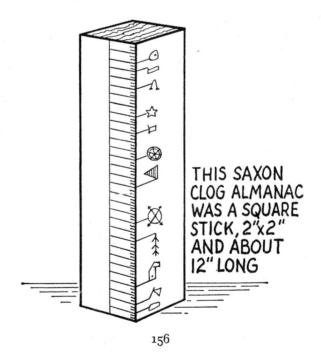

THIS SAXON
CLOG ALMANAC
WAS A SQUARE
STICK, 2"x2"
AND ABOUT
12" LONG

makers went beyond timetables, relating the heavenly happenings to the events of man. They linked the time to sow specific crops with the appearance of certain star formations. Cultural and religious days also were designated with the earliest almanacs. The Romans put their almanacs on blocks of wood measuring eight inches by two inches by two inches. On one long side were the astronomical timetables, and corresponding to these on an adjoining side was the significance of these events. These clog almanacs, as they were called, survived well into the seventeenth century in the British Isles.

The importance of almanacs as literature and to our Western development cannot be emphasized enough. They were considered vital by farmers throughout the Middle Ages when no other calendar, save the heavens themselves, could be depended on. Mariners depended on almanacs for navigation. A manuscript almanac dated 1292 is in the British Museum, which attributes it to Roger Bacon. And Christopher Columbus used an early German almanac for navigation on his voyage to the New World. And the second piece of literature printed by the first American press was *An Almanac Calculated for New England,* by William Pierce, which came off the press right after the *Freeman's Oath* in 1639.

American almanacs, of which there have been hundreds, assumed the role magazines later played in bringing timely information to the public. They contained the astrological charts just as the ancient almanacs did, but these American almanacs went much further in giving weather advice along with native humor and down-home aphorisms. For those of us who think of our forefathers as living in a simple time of clean air and uncluttered lives, almanac reading is indeed an education. For the almanacs are filled with Calvinistic preachments obviously designed to stir farmers faced with a hard life to gainful effort. Ben Franklin, who printed *Poor Richard's Almanac* from 1728 through 1753 under the pseudonym Richard Saunders, certainly epitomizes the emphasis almanac makers placed on attacking laziness, waste, avarice, and the other mortal sins of his age. Such sayings as

"Early to bed, early to rise, makes a man healthy, wealthy, and wise," and "A penny saved is a penny earned," and "God helps those who help themselves," carry the flavor of Franklin's, and all the other almanac makers', preachments.

Few of the moral preachings or the weather lore in these colonial almanacs were original. In Franklin's case, he borrowed heavily from British and French writers for his philosophies and from European almanacs for his weather sayings. This, however, didn't seem to bother the settlers who bought almanacs in quantities second only to Bibles. They depended on these books and took such advice as, "Sow corn when the oak leaves are as big as squirrels' ears," literally. The almanac makers delighted in these backwoods dictates and used them over their own analysis often. This is obvious in the following poem taken from *Poor Robin's Almanac* of 1733:

> Observe which way the hedgehog builds her nest,
> To front the north or south, or east or west;
> For it 'tis true what common people say,
> The wind will blow the quite contrary way.
> If by some secret art the hedgehog knows,
> So long before, the way in which the winds will blow,
> She has an art which many a person lacks
> That thinks himself fit to make our almanacs.

While these books contain a harvest of weather wisdom, they also contain much chaff. The more impressive ones based weather predictions for the coming year on the records of weather for specific dates, on cyclical theories of weather development, and even on sunspot activity. Other almanac writers seemed to use more imagination than mathematics. According to one legend, the *Farmer's Almanac* of 1806 was about to go to press when someone realized that no prediction was made for July 13. The editor was home ill, so a copy boy was sent to get a weather prediction for the missing date. "Put in anything you want," he was told, so the young man inserted, "Rain, hail, and snow." Sure enough, parts of New England had all three on that July 13th.

Poor Richard, 1733

AN

Almanack

For the Year of Christ

1733,

Being the First after LEAP YEAR:

And makes Since the Creation	Years
By the Account of the Eastern Greeks	7241
By the Latin Church, when O ent. r	6932
By the Computation of W.W.	5742
By the Roman Chronology	5682
By the Jewish Rabbies	5494

Wherein is contained

The Lunations, Eclipses, Judgment of the Weather, Spring Tides, Planets Motions & mutual Aspects, sun and Moon's Rising and Setting, Length of Days, Time of High Water, Farm, Courts, and observable Days Fitted to the Latitude of Forty Degrees and a Meridian of Five Hours West from London, but may without Sensible Errors Serve all the Adjacent Places, even from Newfoundland to South Carolina

By *RICHARD SAUNDERS*, Philom.

PHILADELPHIA,

Printed and fold by *B. FRANKLIN*, at the New Printing Office near the Market

Another story is told of the Pennsylvania farmer, who, seeing a meteor shower, was certain the world was ending, so he called to his wife to "quick, bring the Bible." She called back that she couldn't find the Holy Book. "Well, hurry, then, and bring the Almanac," he said. These anecdotes are not far removed from the truth of the near-absolute faith farmers placed in their almanacs. All planting, reaping, building, and butchering was dictated by the information the almanacs provided. Though they were often wrong, belief in them was great, which is probably why Scandinavians reminded themselves who was actually in charge with the saying:

> The almanac writer makes the almanac,
> But God makes the weather.

Part of the delightful flavor of both British and American almanacs has been the wit and native humor of these publications. Almanac makers realized the vulnerability of their forecasts and made it a point to treat themselves and their subjects as lightheartedly as possible. Thus in a passage from the *Old Farmers' Almanac* of 1763 we find the passage:

> The Devil does not know so much of future events, as many expect an almanac maker should foretell; although it must be owned that they are willing to allow him the help of the Devil for his information.

The public joined in on the fun and often chided almanacs for inherent inaccuracies. One story is told about a youth, for instance, who always predicted the weather with uncanny accuracy. When asked how he accomplished this, he said that he was a devoted reader of the almanac, and whatever it predicted for a day, he simply predicted the opposite.

Most almanac predictions, however, did a lot better than chance alone. The *Old Farmers' Almanac*, for example, still boasts of an 80 per cent accuracy average overall since its founding more than 180 years ago. Other almanacs came and went, often basing a reputation on a single lucky guesstimate of a season. Patrick Murphy, for example, was an Irish almanac maker who made his mark by predicting that January 20 would be the coldest day in England in the winter of 1838. It was, and that season became famous as "Murphy's Winter," to which a poem was written:

> Murphy has a weather eye,
>   He can tell whene'er he pleases
> Whether it's wet or whether it's dry,
> Whether it's hot or whether it freezes.

Reading the almanacs makes you forget just how serious the advice in these books was to the farmers and sailors. Robb Sagendorph, in *America and Her Almanacs*, tells of a Boston farmer, Joseph Barrell, who wrote to the *Old Farmers' Almanac* to complain that several predictions for January of 1804 were wrong. There was a severe storm, which developed into a hurricane, on January 8, which the almanac had failed to mention. Barrell's son mailed the letter because Joseph Barrell had been caught by the storm and killed. Such was the life of farmers who placed all of their faith about weather in a single book. William Channing, I believe, captured the essence of that belief when he wrote in *Wanderer* about New Englanders saying:

> Books to them are the faint dreams of students,
>   save that one,
> The battered Almanac, split to the core,
> Fly-blown, and tattered, that above the fire
> Devoted smokes, and furnishes the fates,
> And perigees and apogees of moons.

Beyond reading almanacs to gain both weather wisdom and insight into weather practitioners, I would strongly recommend joining the American Folklore Society. This organization was founded in 1888 and ever since has published a monthly magazine with articles on all aspects of the American lore, written, for the most part, in laymen's English. Most of the articles do not pertain to weather lore, but those that do are well presented and thoroughly documented. Membership in the society is inexpensive and entitles you to receive the monthly *Journal of American Folk-Lore* free. This journal also includes a once-a-year Folklore Bibliography listing virtually all books and articles on lore that have come out during the year. The listings are made by author, title, and subject, which makes for a usable format.

Where else can you look for weather wisdom? How about in the senior branches of your own family tree? It is perhaps a Future Shock symptom of our times that grandparents are daily moving further out of our lives, and with them goes a magnificent hoard of knowledge, eloquent stories of the old ways, and the folk and weather wisdom their grandparents imparted on them. Eliot Wigginton, a high school teacher in Rabun Gap, an isolated Ozark community, realized this wealth when he sent his students home to interview the old-timers. The folklore thus contributed filled a school magazine and later a series of books called *Foxfire*. I believe all American communities could take a lesson from Wigginton and tap this source of old wisdom. At the same time, we might learn something about the aged among us who, like their parents and grandparents before them, contributed a great deal to our science and sensitivities.

Meteorological textbooks, naturally, should be included in your studies as well. There are any number of excellent books dealing with climate and weather forces. I would not venture to recommend one book out of the many, except to say that a text written for private pilots or tyro sailors deals with the elementary facts on the subject, yet at an adult level.

There is a great deal happening in meteorology today that should be of interest. High-speed computers and sophisticated new ground-level sensors coupled with artificial weather satellites are all contributing much to our understanding of weather phenomena. Some fascinating new theories of weather prediction are now in initial test stages and show real promise for truly accurate long-term forecasting. The National Oceanic and Atmospheric Administration, for example, is now measuring the height, speed, and duration of waves in the Gulf of Alaska, which, it is believed, will tell us much about ocean currents and their effect on world weather patterns. Another group experiment, this one called NORPAX (North Pacific Experiment) is measuring the surface temperature of the ocean on the theory that patches of warmer or colder than average sea water produce water-atmosphere heat exchanges that have major influences over the climate of our continent. Several other scientists are now concluding that weather is perhaps most influenced by variations in the jet streams, fast-moving currents of air found in the upper reaches of the troposphere several miles above the earth's surface. Still others are purporting the sunspot theory, that this gaseous activity rises and falls in regular intervals of twenty-two to twenty-three years, affecting our weather directly by these cycles.

Two other theories by leading meteorologists provide a dooms-day tone. Reid Bryson, Director of the Institute for Environmental Studies at the University of Wisconsin, believes that man's industrial and agricultural developments over the past forty years have stirred up a great deal of dust over our planet that will filter sunlight enough to reduce growing seasons. This earth-cooling trend, Bryson contends, will inhibit our ability to feed the world's population. A countertheory comes from Mikhail Budyko of the Soviet Hydrometeorological Service, who believes that the burning of fossil fuels is heating up our atmosphere, not cooling it. Such activity, Budyko concludes, will melt arctic ice and raise the ocean levels to dangerous new heights. And to these conflicting theories you can add the students of weather history who firmly maintain that the weather patterns found in almanacs over the last five hundred years have not changed measurably to this day, in spite of all our industrial activity and exotic new forms of environmental pollution, such as atomic radiation and the carbon monoxide from our sea of cars.

I am not qualified to suggest which of these theoreticians are right, but I would like to express my view by relating a tale from Afghanistan that is some twelve hundred years old. It is about a village judge, Mullah Nazardin, who was called on to try a case. The plaintiff told his side of the story, and Judge Nazardin said,

"Ah, you are right." The defendant then told his side, and Nazardin said, "Ah, *you* are right." The clerk of the court bent down and whispered to the judge, "But, Nazardin, they can't both be right." To which Nazardin replied, "You are right, too."

This ancient anecdote has lasted and is used by many storytellers today. (In fact, I last saw it in a famous play and movie called *Fiddler on the Roof.*) It has survived because it contains a truth many of us tend to forget: Most disputes are not between right and wrong, as in Medieval allegory, but between right and right. All of these influences could be at work in an infinitely varied climatic picture. Each deserves far more consideration before panic or placidity set in.

This may also be the case in the continuing debate between meteorologists and weather lorists over long-term forecasting. Meteorologists say it is impossible to make predictions of more than a few hours or a couple of days with any degree of accuracy. They remind us of Lewis Richardson, a British theoretician who developed the first numerical model for weather forecasting in 1922. Richardson performed calculations for six full weeks in order to make a single twelve-hour global forecast. It was wrong. Since then meteorologists haven't done much better, so those who say long-term forecasting is not yet a reality are actually right. Still, two thousand years ago Aratus was correct in many of his observations of long-term forecasting. Like the Afghanistan anecdote, the ancient weather proverbs have stood the test of time. So to some extent, they must be right, too.

If I may play Nazardin, the judge, for a moment, I would suggest that both sides in the dispute make an effort to recognize the other's rightness. Meteorology is an infant science, which can still learn much from its weather-wise ancestors. And the casual art of weather watching can, and must, gain sophistication from the developing science which will someday become the weather lore of a then-archaic twentieth century. There is much that is right with both meteorological science and weather folklore. There is much we both have to learn to become weather wise, and to someday be able to say, as Shakespeare did in *Antony and Cleopatra:*

> In nature's infinite book of secrecy
> A little I can read.

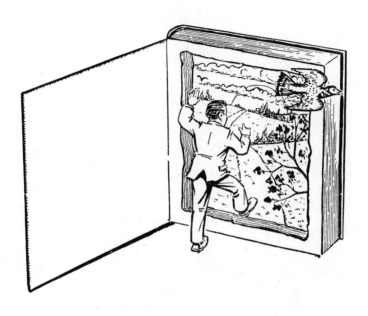

INDEX

Aratus, 45, 52, 54, 56, 61, 67,
68, 84, 91, 119, 127, 153,
164
Prognostica by, 3
Arctic Circle, 14
Aristotle, 35, 76, 93–94, 153
"On Meteors" by, 2
Problems by, 106
Arizona, 5
Arthritis, 40
Ash Wednesday, 151
Assault, 39
Astrologers, 156
Astrological charts, 157
Astronomical timetables, 157
Athens, 109
Atlantic Ocean currents, 104
Atmosphere
cooling theories, 163
heating theories, 163
Atmosphere-water heat exchange,
163
Atmospheric pressure. *See* Air
pressure
Atomic radiation, 163
August, 150
Aurora borealis, 80, 85

Backing wind, 19, 110, 112
Bacon, Francis, *De Sapientia
Veterum* by, 137
Bacon, Roger, 157
Ballad of Sir Patric Spens, 125
Ballot, Buys, 110
Bank of England, 38
Barnabas, St., 149
Barometer, 13, 20, 48
activity of—wind direction—
weather result chart, 111

aneroid, 22, 23
Cape Cod, 23
falling (low pressure, bad
weather), 37, 38, 109
plants as, 52–53
rising (high pressure, good
weather), 37–38, 109
Barrell, Joseph, 161
Bartholomew, St., 138, 150
Bats, 46
Beck, Horace, *Folklore and the
Sea* by, 145
Bedfordshire poem, 12, 130
Bees, 51–52, 56
Behavior
and air pressure, 24, 37, 39
and humidity, 38, 39
and the moon, 116–17
and temperature, 38–39
Benoit, St., 149
Beowulf, 3
Bible, weather references in
Ecclesiastes, 6
Elijah, 36
Exodus, 107
Ezekiel, 107
1 Kings, 36, 90
Job, 3
Jonah, 107
Luke, 106
Matthew, 3
Psalms, 107
Biologists, and birds' storm sen-
sitivity, 9
Birds
air currents and flight, 46
air pressure and flight, 46, 47
migration, 46

167

Rotation
  effects of, 15, 104
  Ferrel's law on, 104
Royal Society, 117
Ruskin, John, 94, 154
Russian saying, 30

Sagendorph, Robb, *America and Her Almanacs* by, 161
Sailors' weather sayings, 81, 82, 90, 91, 93, 95, 96, 99, 104, 118, 119, 131
  See also Mariners
St. Elmo's fire, 80, 86
St. John, Charles, *Wild Sport in the Highlands* by, 45
St. John's Eve, 150
St. Luke's Little Summer, 151
St. Swithin's Day, 11, 150
Saints' days, 137–39, 147–51
Salmon clouds, 93
Salt, 27, 75
Saunders, Richard, 157
Scandinavians, 160
School attendance, 39
Scotland, 78, 79
Sea breeze, 103, 104, 114
Seagulls, 47, 61
Seaweed, 53
Seneca Indians, 81
Senses, 20
  weather effects on, 34, 35
Sensitivity, 2, 34
  storm, 2, 9
September, 150–51
Servatius, St., 138, 149
Shakespeare, William, 3, 153
  Antony and Cleopatra, 165
  Henry IV, 114

King John, 93, 125
Midsummer Night's Dream, 116–17
Richard II, 38
Richard III, 17
Romeo and Juliet, 39, 107
Sonnets, 3, 115
The Tempest, 79, 86, 100
Venus and Adonis, 3–4
Winter's Tale, 72
Sheep, 44, 69
Shelley, Percy Bysshe, 153
  The Cloud by, 90
Shipping industry, 5
Shrove Tuesday, 151
Sight, and weather, 35, 36, 41
Signs of Rain (Jenner), 7–8, 53
Simon, St., 151
Sky, 2, 76–87
  clearing, 91
  color, 3–4, 76–80
  evening-morning predictions, 79–80
  leaden, 17, 96, 97
  mackerel, 18, 95–96, 97
Sky signs, 11, 77–80, 129, 131
Sloane, Eric, 6, 155–56
  Folklore of American Weather by, 156
Smell, sense of, and weather, 35, 36, 41
Smoke, 54–55, 112
Snakes, 56, 58, 104
Snow, 16, 29–32, 63, 135
  predicting, 32
Snow blossoms, 32
Soap bubbles, 55
Society, weather influence on, 34
Sonnets (Shakespeare), 3, 115